Think
DIFFERENTLY

An educator's approach to appreciate what works

Jennifer C. Townsend

Foreword by: Julie Causton

FIRST
Educational Resources

POWERFUL · AFFORDABLE · SUSTAINABLE

Published by:
FIRST Educational Resources, LLC
Winneconne, Wisconsin
www.firsteducation-us.com
info@firsteducation-us.com
ISBN: 978-1-7332390-6-6

Printed in the United States of America
(EnvisionInk Printing Solutions, Neenah, WI)

Author

Jennifer C. Townsend, M.Ed., is an Educational Consultant and the owner of Universal Access Consulting, LLC. Over the past 2 decades, she has worked in collaboration with schools, families, and other professionals to build collective and individual capacity to enhance practices that support the education of individuals with social emotional learning differences including autism spectrum disorder and related disabilities. Jen's work focuses on using appreciative inquiry techniques and social emotional learning practices paired with universal design for learning. She is the co-author of Social Emotional Engagement Knowledge and Skills (SEE-KS), and has been a contributing author to other works including "Social and Emotional Learning Competencies" for the Wisconsin Department of Public Instruction, *A Spectrum of Solutions for Clients with Autism*, along with various blogs and articles. Jen shares knowledge in a manner that educators, families, and other community members can learn from and apply specific to their role and skills. She brings to the field of education her experiences in school and home-based programming, social emotional learning and well-being, universal design for learning, trauma-informed care, professional development, leadership, coaching, and mentorship. Jen has a Master's in Education from Johns Hopkins University in Baltimore, Maryland, received a postgraduate certification in Autism Spectrum Disorder from Johns Hopkins University, and attended University of Wisconsin Eau Claire's Director of Special Education and Pupil Services program. She has also been an adjunct faculty member at Carroll University and Cardinal Stritch University. Jen Townsend is an active member in the field of education and believes that together we can go beyond just *making* a difference; we can *be* the difference.

TABLE OF CONTENTS

Acknowledgements

THINK DIFFERENTLY:

In fact, the first time a platypus was brought from Australia to Britain, people couldn't believe that it was a real animal. They thought that a trickster had sewn two animals together.

(Bradford, 2014)

Persistence is what comes to mind when I consider how this book became a reality. I have many people in my life that believe in me, including myself and those who support me in becoming the best version of me. I want to thank my partner in life for the continuous commitment to being my equal in how we value one another, raise our girls, and share ourselves with each other. I am forever grateful for our relationship, and I know that we are better versions of ourselves because of each other. The graphics in this book are because of your talents, and I thank you for sharing that with the readers too. I sincerely want to thank my daughters for their inspiration. As I watch you two grow and learn each day, you inspire me. You bring so much joy into my life with your creativity, laughter, humor, and continuous curiosity. Thank you both for the support to write this book—specifically for the understanding you gave of time, hugs, jokes, and the ingenious ways to connect with the reader. I love you both endlessly.

I'm also grateful to my reviewers. For the one who took extensive time to go over this work in its draft stages using color coding, comments, appreciation, and a touch of humor: You will forever be remembered by me for this input. To the one who taught me about all the use of quotations, citations, and more. For the one who shared stories with me to ensure that what was written came from a perspective of current happenings in education. To all the educators and learners who crossed paths with me: Your energy, passion, and commitment inspires me each day. Thank you for sharing yourselves and your work with me in a collaborative way. I truly love why I do what I do, especially when we get to grow and learn together. To the one who shared with me how to take the idea of writing a book and make it a reality: I am so grateful for our conversation and your kindness in sharing this gem. To the publisher for offering me the opportunity to put these ideas in a printed version and providing the platform to write this book: I am humbled by each and every one of you. Together, we are doing more than *making* a difference; we are *being* the difference.

THE GARDENER

When a master gardener goes to plant seeds, she looks for variety. She wants a garden full of diverse blooms and rich colors of different heights, widths, hues, and scents. Some tall and showy, shouting "Please look at me!" Others close to the ground, with sparkly earthy warm colors. Some will attract butterflies, others will attract hummingbirds, and still others are simply beautiful to look at. It is the juxtaposition of variation in flower, stem, and foliage that makes the garden breathtaking.

A master gardener knows that beauty is BECAUSE of difference. A master gardener does not find one beautiful flower and measure all other flowers by that one standard flower. She does not only plant hydrangea. She does not determine a flower's value by how close it comes to the standard flower. She doesn't spend time wishing that roses would be less prickly or tulips more hearty. She doesn't wish that sunflowers were shorter. She sees that every single flower has equal parts beauty and limitation. Only by focusing on the beauty can she create the garden in her mind.

A master gardener knows that every flower needs different care. Some need more water, some more sun. Some need to be placed by the edge so they can spread and crawl along the earth, while others like to be close together to create an intricate root system. Some need well-drained rocky soil, and others need dark rich soil. All weeds need to be cleared. A master gardener understands this and carefully considers the needs of each when creating a garden for everyone.

This is not only a book about the flowers and appreciating their beauty. It is also a book about the gardener. This book requires that we search for and nurture the good in ourselves in order to be truly inspired gardeners. This book helps us to get our tools in order. This book helps us arrange our tools so that we can find what is best about every single flower and nurture it. This book is about how to be the very best gardener for the beautiful and unique plants in our care.

This book goes against the culture of normalcy in schools. I can think of no better book for educators to read than a book about valuing difference—not tolerating or accepting difference, not about measuring students against a cultivated standard, but instead truly valuing what is unique about everyone to create the most magnificent garden with the potential for unknowable growth.

I am proud to announce this book to you. Jen Townsend and her team of administrators introduced Appreciative Inquiry to me, and I find it to be one of the most valuable tools in my own tool bucket as I help to create profoundly inclusive schools. This magnificent book will provide an opportunity to see through the lens of appreciation as we approach both the flower and you, my dear, the gardener.

Julie Causton, Ph.D.

THINK DIFFERENTLY:

Platypuses swim with their front feet and steer with their
tails and back feet. While in the water, their waterproof
fur works as a skin to cover their ears, eyes, and noses,
sealing them shut to protect the animal while underwater.

(Bradford, 2014)

For the love of learning

Have you ever heard the brain referred to as a computer? It's as if to say
that we operate in our day-to-day lives with something resembling hard-
ware and software. The term *neuroplasticity* has been used to describe
the organ protected inside our skull since it was coined in the late 1800s
by psychologist William James. But what if instead, we think differently
and consider the brain to be a living, ever-evolving organ that is "livewired" and continuously developing in various ways? Neuroscientist
David Eagleman has described the brain's functioning as if all of its experiences shape it; it's "livewired." If we think of the brain as plastic and
entertain the concept of neuroplasticity, we can imagine it being shaped
and formed differently; however, once it has been molded, it has to be
re-melted and re-molded in order to change again. Is that what we are
hoping to do—shape and reshape the brain? What if, instead, our goal

is to develop and "grow" the neural pathways in our brain? Eagleman (2020) encapsulated this different way of thinking by saying the "magic of our brain lies not in its constituent elements but in the way those elements unceasingly reweave themselves to form a dynamic, electric, living fabric" (p. 16). In this book, we will go on a journey together to discover more about this view of learning and how to appreciate what works. Together, we will embrace the idea of thinking differently. On your mark, get set, action!

Appreciate you

Most books begin with writing about "why," saving the "how" until later. By joining me on this journey, however, you are choosing to think differently, so let's adjust that traditional model. If this feels a bit odd for you, that's okay. We have kept the book in the "why, what, and how" sequence, yet the "why" and "what" are brief, as we know the "how" of our work is where we will want to spend the most time. Consider using the table of contents to read the book in a way that fits your learning preference. It is divided into three parts for this exact reason. There is no wrong way to read this book, so long as you reach your goal of why you opened this cover and started reading.

Ask yourself: how do I want to engage with this book?

> Will I follow it page for page? Will I highlight the text? Will I dog ear the pages? Will I read it with a peer(s)? Will I flip to the end for the appendices? Will I use the table of contents to read it in a different order than it is written?

I will engage with this book by …

Let's take a quick moment to frame our thinking so that we can truly engage with this text. I invite you to think about moments when you worked to "fix" a situation, rather than to "notice" the situation. For example, imagine a child getting some jam on his shirt while eating. He then chooses to use a wet cloth to clean it, and ends up with a large wet spot of smeared jam on the shirt. An adult approaches the situation by saying, "Go put on a new shirt." Rather unexpectedly, the child politely says, "Why would I do that, when I can just put on my favorite scarf until it is dry? Besides, I like the color purple." At times, it may feel that we need to fix what might not be ours to fix.

Have you ever found yourself in a similar situation of offering a solution to others' perceived problems? Such suggestions are often well-intended, yet sometimes we offer unsolicited fixings when our role should instead be to:

- Empathize, not solve
- Propose, not expect
- Offer, not demand
- Ask, not tell
- Listen, not talk at
- Show kindness, not just politeness

We appreciate one another and ourselves when we do the former, rather than the latter. Simon Sinek (2019), author of *Start with Why*, indicated, "The amount of openness, patience, curiosity and compassion that I hold for myself will be directly reflected in my behavior (actions) with others." Now, with all this in mind, let us embark on this journey to learn the finesse of appreciating what works in our practices in order to enhance it.

Notice what works

As we learn the art of appreciation, we will discover the good qualities of a situation. Naturally, it seems easier to identify flaws or bad qualities; however, by learning the finesse of appreciation, we disrupt our traditional thinking patterns to immerse ourselves into the opportunity to think differently. I remember watching myself in a video reading a story to my daughter. The first thought I had was, "Goodness, what was I thinking with that outfit, and why was I sitting on a chair while my daughter was on the floor?" By doing this, I didn't even notice my daughter, who was 2 years old at the time, pointing to a bird on the bird-feeder and saying, "Mommy look, bird." At her age, she wanted to share all about what she was seeing and what she noticed in her environment which may have not been what I wanted her to do. At that moment, we were reading the book *Brown Bear Brown Bear* by Eric Carle, and I was recording it because I was getting ready to travel and wanted her to have this video while I was gone for 2 nights. When I looked back at the video, prior to honing my skills of appreciative noticing, I saw the negative. I saw that she was not paying attention. She was distracted, looking out the window and not at the book. Initially being unable to notice what was working, I missed all the good qualities in this moment. These good qualities being that she was seeing things in her environment, sharing her experiences, pointing to a real bird, connecting her life with litera-ture. "Brown Bear, Brown Bear, what do you see?" Have you ever looked at a video of yourself, and the first thought was negative? Yes, I am sure we all have at some point in our lives. I recognize that it can be extremely challenging to discover what's working. It takes finesse and an understanding of engage-ment to notice what works.

"How will I remind myself to appreciate the moment?"

Engagement, otherwise known as the *why* of learning—the hook, the motiva-tion to learn—is different for each of us. It is directly connected to our affective networks in the brain. These enable us to focus, to sustain effort and persistence through the use of motivation and emotional connection to the opportunity. This idea of engagement is interesting when you consider how you are engaging with this book. You were given some ideas, and you figured it out for yourself. You knew why it would work for you. Do you remember the question asked earlier in this chapter about how you want to engage with this book? Maybe you answered it. Maybe you skipped it and are now thinking, "Why did I skip it?" Either way, I encourage you to stop, reflect, and truly challenge yourself to answer the question, "How do I want to engage with this book?" Let me offer some ideas to encourage you to write a response. Grab a sticky-note and put it on this page with your answer. Get a pencil and lightly write your response in the margin on this page. Motivate yourself to write something down. CAST (2018) researchers have discovered that some learners are highly engaged by spontaneity and novelty, while others are disengaged, even frightened, by those aspects, preferring strict routine. Some learners might like to work alone, while others prefer to work with their peers. In reality, there is no one means of engagement that will be optimal for all learners in all contexts. We want to value ourselves, the reader, as the learner. We will want to think differently than we may have in the past as we embark on this learning journey together. We will want to dig into our own learning preferences and truly value ourselves as we discover what works.

"What is my purpose in reading this book?"

I am so glad that you are already beginning to appreciate yourself. By responding to how you want to engage in this book, you are appreciating your time and your learning. You will not waste any time reading information in a prescribed way, if that does not work for you. You are choosing to engage in a way that will work for you. So, why do we ask our learners to engage with content in a way that may not work for them? Instead, why not present the broader idea of what we hope they get from the learning? Then, we could invite them to discover how to engage in their own way—a way that works for them. We could offer a bit of support with autonomy when needed, but a child's learning is not a problem to be fixed. Rather, it is an opportunity to notice what works and enhance those moments. I encourage you to use some self-talk when you are tasked with the idea of fixing someone by saying to yourself, "It is not my role to fix someone; rather, it is my role to notice what works." In this book, we will hone our skills of noticing to enhance our daily practices through appreciation. I believe that by the end of this book, you will think differently. Together, we can make all the difference.

Part I
WHY

THINK DIFFERENTLY:
Although a platypus is born out of a leathery egg, the babies nurse from their mothers.

(Bradford, 2014)

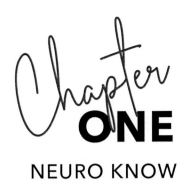

ONE

NEURO KNOW

Why Falling in Love with the Social World is Critical to Learn

The basics of social neuroscience and your amygdala too

So, if we go with the idea that the brain is constantly changing, and we know—thanks to Vygotsky—that the brain tends to do better when it's in the "zone of proximal development," maybe we can enhance our practices through the use of appreciation, rather than judgment or unsolicited expertise. Dr. Judi Willis (2006), a neuroscientist and educator, shared that the amygdala gets highly active when a person is in a state of stress, causing the lower 80% of the brain to respond with either fight, flight, or freeze. Neuroscanning of someone in a bored state—that is, out of their learning zone—shows that the amygdala is in a heightened state of arousal. So, let's not bore or stress our brains; take a look at Figure 1.1 to stimulate another part of it.

Figure 1.1 Comfort, Learning, and Panic Zones

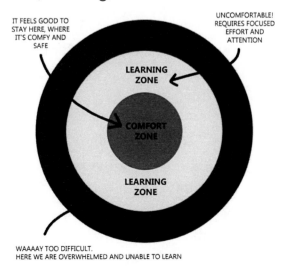

In his daily insights on life and habits, Dr. Jud Brewer (2020) addressed the various zones and places emphasis on the individual's mindset being a direct predictor of a person's ability to embrace challenges, get curious with mistakes, appreciate effort, and continue in the learning journey. Yet, if we frequently find ourselves in the comfort zone, we are too safe. We need to become comfortable with the uncomfortable through the exploration of our skills. We need to sustain effort and focus attention to be expert learners who fuel the brain to grow.

Finding the spark

Resilience and hope—the social neuroscience that we all need to spark the drive for new learning—comes from the emotional part of the brain. When people are together and socially connected, endorphins are released in the brain, which provides a "craving" for more, enticing us to focus our attention, address challenges, and persist in sustained effort. Our intrinsic motivation to learn increases when we make an emotional connection to subject matter (Whitman & Kelleher, 2016). We increase self-efficacy when we are connected through social engagement, the "fuel" for our brains to grow through relationships. Emotion and social connectedness are inseparable from learning. The amygdala, found in the limbic system, is the live-wiring station for our emotions which drives our investment, our independence, and our output of learning. Together, we will find the value in stimulating our amygdala through the use of a positive psychology approach. We will use appreciation to engage in our own learning and the learning of others with whom we feel socially connected.

Amplifying the social emotional engagement in learning can be a very personal experience for all learners—including *you*, the reader. It can make us feel vulnerable, yet we know that in order to develop and become an expert learner, we too must invest and take action. We can do this by supporting one another through mentorship and discovering ways to provide opportunities for all learners to access, engage and express themselves within their learning. In this regard, Dr. Willis (2007) expressed the importance of thinking about varying learning opportunities specific to the individual by "determining their achievable challenge level, the zone of proximal development" (p. 29). Judy emphasized the need for intrinsic motivation that gets the dopamine going; not the sticker reward, but rather the "Ah! I got it!" that lights up the brain and ignites the curiosity in learning. It is when we connect moments like this with our social engagement that we generate the sparks that ignite the "fuel" that makes the brain grow.

TAKE THIS OPPORTUNITY TO CONSIDER:

Who do I trust and value as a colleague that I would consider entering a mentorship relationship?

That's not to say all learners experience the same pattern of brain activation, though. Neuroimaging has shown that children with social emotional differences tend to process social stimuli in regions typically used for processing images and sounds that are non-social. These differences may compromise an intrinsic desire to engage in classroom activities and may make predicting the actions, intentions, and emotions of others inefficient (Chevallier et al., 2012). As social and emotional engagement increases, the costly challenges associated with disengagement decrease. It would be delightful if we could simultaneously decrease self-doubt, depression, low self-worth, and negative self-talk, all while feeling good about ourselves and those we support through our relationships, our families, and our careers. We can do this by discovering how to love our amygdala and appreciate our own knowledge and skills to fuel our brains to engage and grow.

"How I react and respond to these differences generates a positive sense of self and belonging."

What happens when we think differently? Some educators' perspectives hinge on this question for exploration: *What if learning activities appreciate and celebrate the differences each of us brings and also guide us to find commonalities that support an intrinsic desire to engage, feel valued and have a sense of belonging?* You'll notice a reference to the "3i's" of engagement (investment, independence, and initiation) included in the table below. We'll explore them in more detail later in the book. Right now, this is an example to support us in finding the spark in designing the learning experiences.

UDL Guidelines and the "3i's" of Engagement
The WHY, WHAT & HOW of Learning
Learner Investment, Independence & Initiation

Community Conversations

A time to come together and build relationships by sharing about oneself. An opportunity where learners have the option to share, comment, or "pass" by choosing *why to*, *what to*, and *how to* engage in the experience.

Goal of Community Conversation

Given access to classmates, sentence starters such as "I notice when...," "I feel...," "When I see..., I think...," etc., visuals to display the discussion and a question for consideration, the learners will share their perspectives and passions. Learners will engage by managing impulsivity, seeking to understand and connect with peers by using active listening, and contributing respectful comments or questions for the duration of the community conversation.

Educator provides options for learners to access

On the whiteboard, chart paper, or with technology, a visual is shared to capture the conversation. Notes are written to scribe the community conversation discourse.

Side note: *The notes shall not take away from the conversation rather will serve as a visual rendition of the auditory information shared.*

- The educator may provide a reflective prompt to initiate thinking and awareness such as, "I am noticing Edward has shared multiple times and I'm wondering who else wants to be heard." Sometimes the conversation may stall. When this occurs, an educator may choose to inquire by saying, "I'm wondering if someone wants to propose the next question to continue the conversation."

Side note: At times questions may stall. This may be due to the learners' interest, current events or maybe because it has struck a chord. It's okay. It will happen. Pivot if needed.

Educator provides opportunities for learners to build

- The community conversation questions initially developed by the educator and gradually released to the learners over time.

Side note: the gradual release will provide insights into who the learners are and may give perspective on their backgrounds, interests, cultural experiences, and social connection.

- In the discourse note taking, review the whole group's impulsivity and identify strategies that will support learners to sustain effort and persistence.

- Consider developing signals for expression to give learners who may otherwise vocalize their thinking a way to share but not disrupt the flow.

Side note: The hand gesture with your pinkie and thumb pointing outward while the other fingers are folded down and shifting back and forth may signal "I'm thinking that too" or "I'm connecting to what you're saying."

- Learners may notice the cause-and-effect or ramification of how our actions affect others and evaluate how we can best support our own actions or reactions through responsible decision-making.

Side note: learners' may recognize where they choose to sit, who is nearby, their eating habits, sleeping habits or other variables that can affect how they listen, their thoughts, expressions, mindset, and the impact on their engagement.

Educator provides resources for learners to internalize

- Visuals provide the opportunity to reflect on, notice, and note what worked within our community. These visuals also provide a record of community conversations and can be synthesized by noticing patterns for improvement, trends throughout the weeks or months, recall of the conversations as well as how the experiences made us feel.

Side note: this creates the opportunity for learners to internalize experiences that may grow their regulation skills, comprehension and executive functions in strategy development, management of information and generalization of this learning experience.

- Consider opportunities as a community to re-approach learners who may have "passed." To recognize and honor their decisions. To provide the opportunity but not push to ensure that we continue to cultivate and develop a safe space to share without judgment where all learners feel a sense of belonging.

Side note: as learners begin to see peers or notice within themselves opportunities to initiate in the community circle, the number of "pass" responses decrease the more we engage in this style of learning.

Learners are purposeful and motivated, as noticed by their investment

- Learners select—with educator-scaffolded supports and prior reflections—the questions for the community circle.

- Learners explore how we pass the speaker role to bring awareness and collaboration to provide opportunities for all voices to be heard.

- Learners notice when peers have offered their thoughts through sharing, passing, or seemingly disinterested in the topic and may offer to pose another question as time allows.

Learners are resourceful and knowledgeable, as noticed by their independence

- Learners select seating spots within the community circle with consistency. Visual reminders for "When selecting a community circle spot, I can ask myself: 'Will this spot enhance my focus to learn more about myself and my peers?', 'Will this spot enhance my active listening?', or 'Will this spot support my management of impulsivity?'"

- Learners remember to take their community circle index card with phrases or sentence starters if desired.

- Learners select a focus object, if needed, to support their sustained attention yet choose an item that will not deter from the focus of the community circle experience.

Learners are strategic and goal-directed, as noticed by their initiations

- Learners raise their hand or share a post-it note with a community circle question they would like to ask the group.
- Learners use signals developed by the group to show connections to peers' comments.
- Learners Commenting sentence starters and phrases are provided on index cards or community circle anchor charts as a visual reference tool.

Connections:

Perspective-taking is when we share about who we are and what matters to us. Through this process, we learn about how and when to share. This can be leveraged in our content and instructional planning to support how we process and reflect shared experiences, common goals as readers, in mathematics, as scientists, and across other content areas. When possible engage in "share-outs" after core-content classes to recognize these connections.

When we share our process, our learning and our takeaways, we are also connecting to the social emotional learning competencies of self awareness, self management, social awareness, relationship skills and responsible decision making as we continue in the journey of becoming expert learners.

Side note: as learners we reflect on our engagement by asking ourselves and thinking about the community's collective responses to appreciate active listening and a sense of connectedness.

Educator Reflection:

Both as an educator and a learner, we found opportunities to enrich and extend relationships, discourse and build a social identity. Each week we departed one another with our belonging questions such as: "Did I feel that my voice had a place and a space in our community conversation?", "Did I feel like I belong?", "Did I feel my perspective brought value?", "Did I choose to share or pass?", and "Did I accept that my actions were what was best for me today?"

We used the survey to gather our data, so we could better understand our engagement. Our goal of 100% of our classmates will feel like they belonged, were valued and chose to share their voice and perspectives. Our percentages started small, grew, dipped and jumped as we experienced ups and downs just like we all do in life. We noticed when we dipped and why that might be. We celebrated and felt proud when our percentages may have skyrocketed and spent time determining why and how to maintain and sustain. We even met our goal of 100% several times!

Time Duration for Community Conversation 15 - 20 minutes

When people make an emotional connection to the subject matter, it increases their intrinsic motivation and investment in the learning (Whitman & Kelleher, 2016). We often assume that others have similar experiences and tend to surround ourselves with like-minded individuals. Indeed, we—intentionally or unintentionally—pass judgment on others who are different from us, and at times we fail to appreciate one another or even ourselves. When we do, our brain begins to generate its response based on the precedents of our neurodevelopment and prior experiences. The role of an educator, parent, colleague, friend, or as a generally good human being is to support one another, as well as to guide learning through consideration, appreciation, and collaboration.

TAKE THIS MOMENT TO PAUSE.

Consider a time when you might have fallen in or out of love with the social world. Or, maybe reflect about a time when you intentionally or unintentionally passed judgment.

When a person's social brain has fallen in love with people, developed a high rate of communication, and acquired language about others and their actions, that person will likely develop the ability to plan ahead to maintain relationships over time. This, along with the depth and complexity of development, allows the person to figure out the necessary social rules to interact with friends, to be a teammate, and to develop long-term relationships. These are the "skills" of social competence, and we do this by providing the brain with a chemical cocktail of dopamine, oxytocin, and other endorphins (Rubin et al., 2015). As an educator or caregiver, you can make a positive impact on social development and foster that delightful chemical cocktail through appreciation, discussion, and intentional teaching of the "3i's" skills.

THINK DIFFERENTLY

TWO

NEUROPLASTICITY

Why Social Neuroscience is Valuable for Educators to Understand

The effects of an appreciative approach

Social development directly and inevitably affects us all. Social development consists of seeking out social connections, using language—both verbal and nonverbal—to connect with others, and ultimately "falling in love" with the social world. Some connect with others through the social world, and this enhances social development. Others seemingly tend not to connect with how society defines the social world, may have inhibited the use of language to connect with others, and end up not yet seeking out traditional social connections, connecting instead to objects or activities with more predictability. These individuals may not readily develop or have already fallen out of love with the social world. Here's where professionals usually step in to support and set up strategies.

Often professionals do things *to* the individual, not *with* the individual. While well-intentioned, they try to "fix it" rather than appreciate where the individual is at the moment and grow from there. Appreciative inquiry is a positive inquiry-based approach that focuses on what's working, rather than seeking to fix what's wrong. By using an inquiry-based process within a multidisciplinary team approach, the participants tend to demonstrate empathy towards one another's point of view. The purpose of supporting with empathy and not demanding goes back to the idea of thinking differently. If we provide one another with the feeling of safety and a sense of belonging, there's a strong likelihood we will actively seek out, plan ahead, and maintain relationships with others over time.

When we provide support, it is crucial to place the emphasis on the "skills" of social competence with strong consideration towards how we want to directly teach the skill and the ways in which this skill supports investment, independence, or initiation. Consider the following scenario:

"How am I choosing to show up?"

> *James is a learner with ASD and anxiety disorder. He has seemingly done well in school, although upon entering the upper grade levels in school, his self-advocacy has become a challenge for educators to manage. James adamantly refuses to complete school assignments and comments that his teachers are disorganized and have minimal content knowledge. James also shared that he detests having to document his thinking. He does not turn in assignments, projects, or coursework. The teachers note that James does not complete his work, and that James frequently tells them that he knows how to do it but dislikes any adult telling him what to do. His teachers also share that James does not seem to have friendships. His parents agree that he does not have strong friendships (though they acknowledge he does have some acquaintances), but they do not see this adamant refusal to complete tasks at home. They see a smart young man who wants to get good grades, go to college, and become an engineer. Based on this information, the Individualized Educational Planning (IEP) team feels that James needs more structure to breakdown the work assignments, as they are an important part of his grades [and] suggests that he use an agenda book to help him keep track of his due dates for assignments, just like he manages his time to study for exams, so he can submit them in a timely manner.*

(Bedard & Hecker, 2020, p. 127)

Consider the skills of social competence and the IEP team's decision about using an agenda. As mentioned, the team decides to have James use an agenda, but he finds the projects assigned by his teacher to be completely pointless. Why would completing an agenda book be important to him if he can ace the exams? In talking further with James about how he would benefit from the use of self-monitoring tools and self-talk to guide his behavior, the team could have discovered that he likes to learn by sharing facts, observations, and self-directed instruction, not collaboration or doing "busy work." Therefore, rather than telling James to use an agenda book to organize his projects, the team could have used an appreciative process to discover, dream, design, and deliver a viable solution by

1. Considering his current skills in self-management;

2. Discovering how he manages his time to study for exams;

3. Modeling and/or discussing a variety of self-monitoring tool options for him to observe;

4. Creating a clear understanding for why goal-setting and organizational skills are critical to his future aspirations; and

5. Letting James take the lead in the delivery for how this will look for projects.

We do all of this with the understanding that if it does not work, we will make some adjustments based on the principles of appreciative inquiry.

In further conversations with James, it may become evident that he had not considered others' perspectives and did not realize there was more to getting a good grade than assessment scores. By appreciating his current skills and providing James a voice in the outcome, the team could have found a collaborative solution that was logical and supported social competence skills in organization. The teachers also would have learned that fewer projects and more opportunities for James to show his knowledge on exams, tests, and quizzes would support their relationship and enhance the opportunities for him to feel success across a range of social settings.

It is important to note that James needed to feel valued (i.e., invested) in the conversation in order to be engaged in implementing the solution. It was helpful to define the problem and narrow it down with specific discrete examples so that all parties involved communicated their perceptions. In our own practice, the goal is for the individuals to understand each other's perceptions about the identified problem and then develop a solution that is led by the learner (i.e., James) rather than the adults (i.e., the IEP team). To do this, we need to provide support with empathy for James and guide the team to think differently about their approach.

Digging a bit deeper into the appreciative approach

So, if we can do this when we think about a learner we support, why would we stop there? We can think differently about how we mentor one another and use an appreciative inquiry process to discover, dream, design, and deliver an enhanced version of something that is already working, while enabling others to feel appreciated and valued in the process. H. Jackson Brown Jr. (2007), a best-selling author of many books about life and love, posited that "A person's greatest emotional need is to feel appreciated" (p. 41). This quote reminds us about why using appreciative inquiry might feel like the "missing piece" in education. In an effort to feel positive about our practices, the use of an appreciative inquiry approach can be a critical factor to feeling energized about creating a collective and positive impact.

> How will you support someone to recognize and develop skills in social competence?

If we again consider the James scenario and the idea of "fueling the brain to grow," we will want to start with a common goal, such as creating a parallel project to appreciate James's learning preference, and then model it for him to observe. For instance, James and the professional would:

- First, both make their own project to be shared with others.

- Then, seek out others to share the project with, being sure to co-create sentence starters and organizational structures for the social exchange such as "I selected this word/image because ___" or "I feel this picture describes me when _____."

- Finally, they would share this with other individuals across home, school, and community environments, as feasible and appropriate for the context.

It is important to note that sometimes we ask individuals to share their personal selves with us, yet they do not know anything about us, which makes it a bit one-sided. Only when diverse perspectives are included, respected, and valued can we start to get a full picture of the world: who we serve, what they need, and how to successfully meet people where they are (Adie et al., 2018). Challenge yourself to think differently about those we support and to appreciate where the learner is in the moment. Consider where we enter their lives—not their past and not yet their future—to appreciate the here and now. Recognize that we are all different, and that is what makes us unique in our professions. We can do more than make a difference when we believe in our collaborative efforts. Together, we can be the difference. This writing is meant to challenge you to think differently, to be brave, to grow, and to nurture yourself and those you appreciate.

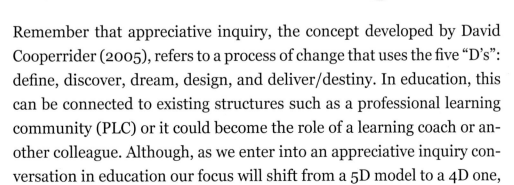

"Meeting others where they are will support others to meet me where I am right now."

Remember that appreciative inquiry, the concept developed by David Cooperrider (2005), refers to a process of change that uses the five "D's": define, discover, dream, design, and deliver/destiny. In education, this can be connected to existing structures such as a professional learning community (PLC) or it could become the role of a learning coach or another colleague. Although, as we enter into an appreciative inquiry conversation in education our focus will shift from a 5D model to a 4D one, as we will have already defined our purpose for inquiry. In education our focus will be on discovering, dreaming, designing, and delivering. Our work is to shift from a deficit-based model of problem-solving team discussions to a constructionist-based model in which we use the art of appreciation to discover the best of what *is*, imagine what *might be*, dialog what *could be*, and create what *will be*.

Figure 2.1 Variations in Approach

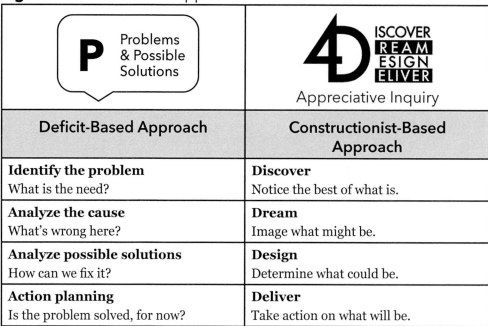

Deficit-Based Approach	Constructionist-Based Approach
Identify the problem What is the need?	**Discover** Notice the best of what is.
Analyze the cause What's wrong here?	**Dream** Image what might be.
Analyze possible solutions How can we fix it?	**Design** Determine what could be.
Action planning Is the problem solved, for now?	**Deliver** Take action on what will be.

Appreciative inquiry as a positive psychology method of mentorship begins by identifying what is already working towards our desired outcomes and supporting the mentee by inquiring about where they see opportunities to take action. At the individual level, mentorship might involve having an educator mentor another educator, a parent mentor another parent, or a healthcare professional mentor another healthcare professional. This peer-to-peer format is ideal, as we are simply noticing what interactive and learning supports appear to be fostering engagement, rather than critiquing or evaluating them. If the mentorship is used by an instructional coach with an educator or a social worker with a parent, it will be important that one's role as a "mentor" during this particular process is identified upfront so that the mentee is comfortable being observed and supported. It all flows back to loving your amygdala;

we enter the panic zone when our emotions are stressed.

The goal is for professionals, families, and community members alike to be lifelong learners. There will be moments when an expertise is a strength and other times when a skill is emerging, but not yet developed. These are the times in which we need to actively seek out information in a manner that works best for us.

I appreciate you

Truly, this process is all about appreciation and how we value ourselves in our practices. Dale Carnegie's (1937) *How to Win Friends and Influence People* is a resource that continues to hold true today. I challenge you to reflect upon this quote: "The difference between appreciation and flattery? That is simple. One is sincere and the other insincere. One comes from the heart out; the other from the teeth out. One is unselfish; the other selfish. One is universally admired; the other universally condemned" (Carnegie, 1937, p. 26). At times, these differences in approach will vastly impact our lives. Curiously, I wonder how this applies to your life.

Consider a comment you said to someone. Was it appreciation or flattery?

1. Write the comment here:
2. Consider the following questions.

Was my intention sincere?	Was there something in it for me?
Was my comment genuine?	Was it said because that's what I thought the other person wanted to hear?
Was it connected to an action?	Was it said in a fake manner?
Was it shared in a positive light?	Was it said with a negative tone?
Column A	**Column B**

If you answered more in Column A, you're discovering the art of appreciation.

If your comment was more in Column B, you're tending to use flattery.

Recognizing the intention in comments will support the conscious use of appreciation. It is an art, and it may take time to nurture this skill. The challenge is to demonstrate this art of appreciation across various experiences and in different situations. To do this, we must stay well and stay curious as we continue to invite others to join us in noticing and wondering, to empathize, not solve, and remain compassionate for ourselves and others. According to a well-informed yoga leader, "When we truly get to know ourselves and respect ourselves, I truly believe the world is a better place." (Yoga with Adriene, 2019). Together, we can share appreciation and truly respect ourselves in the process.

Part II
WHAT

THINK DIFFERENTLY:

The bill of a platypus, sometimes called a duck-billed platypus, has a smooth texture that feels like suede. It is also flexible and rubbery. The skin of the bill holds thousands of receptors that help the platypus navigate underwater and detect movement of potential food, such as shrimp.

(Bradford, 2014)

Chapter THREE

THE ELEMENTS

What We Value in Expert Learners and the "3i's" of Engagement

The elements that make a positive impact

There is a vast number of resources that you can apply during your journey to think differently. It is valuable to understand that what you are doing is not something new; rather, it is honing a skill that you already possess. It is making meaningful connections and braiding initiatives together. It is applying the concept that the brain is 'livewired' and ever-evolving, growing, and learning based on what we chose to do.

It is my hope that you think about your collective knowledge and apply what you know into the skills that will be shared in the "how" part of this book. When we consider ourselves as learners and ask the question, "What do we value in learners?" we discover the "3i's" of engagement: investment, independence, and initiation. These skills correlate with education-based learning standards, as well as CASEL's Social Emotional Learning (SEL) competencies; they also align to the Universal Design for Learning (UDL) guidelines. Before we dive in, let's calibrate to ensure we have similar working definitions of a few concepts.

"What do you value in learners?"

Universal Design for Learning (UDL) is defined by CAST as *a*

framework to improve and optimize teaching and learning for all people based on scientific insights into how humans learn. In the appendices, you will find the UDL guidelines and I encourage you to explore this framework deeply and continuously (CAST, 2018).

Social Emotional Learning (SEL) is defined by CASEL as an integral part of education and human development. SEL is the process through which all young people and adults acquire and apply the knowledge, skills, and attitudes to develop healthy identities, manage emotions, achieve personal and collective goals, feel and show empathy for others, establish and maintain supportive relationships, and make responsible and caring decisions (CASEL, 2017). The appendices also include CASEL's SEL competencies for your further investigation.

The **Social Emotional Engagement - Knowledge and Skills (SEE-KS)** model includes ways to enhance dissemination of social neuroscience related to the social and emotional development in children, empowering multidisciplinary teams to support students by using the most effective instructional strategies, and fostering learner engagement, including investment, independence, and initiation through an appreciative inquiry approach (Rubin et al., 2014). In the appendices, you will be able to locate many of the tools mentioned, and I hope you check them out.

KNOWLEDGE AND SKILLS

Knowledge: The fact or condition of knowing something with familiarity gained through experience or association.

Skills: The ability to use one's knowledge effectively and readily in execution or performance.

Per Merriam-Webster Dictionary

Investment in Learning

Investment is the "why" of engagement. Our "social connectedness." It is the learner motivation that provides purpose for engagement in learning.

Independence in Learning

Independence is the "what" of engagement. Our resourcefulness. It is the learning fluency that provides access for engagement in learning.

Initiation in Learning

Initiation is the "how" of engagement. Our actions to share information with others. It is the expression that provides desire for engagement in learning.

These definitions focus on the "fluency of learning," and our work is to enhance the "3i's" of engagement through collaboration. We will do this by adjusting the learning environment when there are opportunities to strengthen one of the "3i's" of engagement. Our goal is to identify the opportunities to strengthen these skills and enhance what works. The rationale for why this is so important becomes so much stronger when we align our thinking with UDL and also have an understanding of the learning brain. A CAST (2018) report delineated the brain into three brain networks specifically:

- Affective networks, or the WHY of learning focusing on engagement
- Recognition networks, or the WHAT of learning focusing on representation
- Strategic networks, or the HOW of learning focusing on action and expression

When we place an emphasis on engagement, representation, and expression in our teaching practices, the rationale for promoting the "3i's" of engagement for learners becomes more consequential. Let's take a look at the connection and consider how this may look.

ĭnvestment

Investment is the "why" of engagement. Our "social connectedness." It is the learner motivation that provides purpose for engagement in learning.

Specifically, we can consider how to foster investment for learners. Prompts that can be used to take a deeper look at learner interests being incorporated into the learning experiences might be to ask yourself,

- "Are hands-on materials available?"
- "Is learning connected to real-life applications?"
- "Has choice been given?"
- "Are there routines in the learning?"
- "Were peer partners considered and meaningfully selected?"
- "Will visual supports be available throughout the learning experience?"

When these prompts and these ideas are incorporated in our design, we enhance the learner investment and notice higher levels of learner engagement.

To stimulate interest and support learner regulation strategies, consider:

- Pairing complex language with activities that have a clear application to daily life and real-life materials (e.g., learning fractions as they relate to baking bread or making a favorite family recipe)
- Embedding relevant themes and learner interests into activities (e.g., videographer, reporter, social media influencer, etc.)
- Providing choices of topics, materials, and the product being created (e.g., write a story, create a podcast, or design a mural)
- Providing opportunities for social connections (e.g., interacting with preferred partners, role play, competition, or small group collaboration)

THINK DIFFERENTLY

- Embedding discussion, examples, or modeling prior to activities as to what might be helpful when in need of assistance or unsure of expectations

- Providing visuals, peer models, and hands-on materials for learners to choose regulation strategies

- Providing visuals and role models for learners to express emotion, remorse, and negotiate with others (e.g.," I wasn't expecting this today, can we do____ or _____ instead?")

- Providing tools for learners to recognize their level of engagement in an activity, identify strategies that might sustain engagement, and self-advocate

"What am I already doing to ensure learners' investment?"

A glimpse into a collaborative classroom follows:

It's time for a new unit, now what? How can we leverage learners' engagement to ensure investment throughout the learning?

In our collaborative classroom, we worked towards content learning and understanding through a multidisciplinary approach. We entered a new unit that focuses on becoming an expert learner. To become an expert, we will engage in solving and investigating problems that currently exist, as a meteorologist, while reading and processing informational text, writing, and constructing an informative product such as an essay.

The plans are set. The collaboration is solid. The ideas are ready to be shared with learners. Then along came a passionate learner who gave us the opportunity to facilitate his learning and grow our knowledge and skills as educators. Let's meet Kevin.

Kevin's investment into this unit was anchored on his passion for technology and camera work. It started by thinking differently about how he and others can use their strengths and curiosity to drive their learning—all while also sustaining focus and effort to help guide their process, participation, and success along the way. For Kevin, this opportunity was recording and reporting, incorporating his passion into learning, and creating an informative product—but maybe not an essay just yet.

We recognized his passion, we hooked his interest, and from what we can tell, he seems connected, but how we design the learning and plan for including his interests as a means to stimulate investment and motivation AND teach the content all while providing support for sustaining this engagement in developmentally appropriate ways is the opportunity.

Here's how we approached it.

Initially, Kevin began by using technology to record the reading and writing shared during our lecture (whole-group lesson). The purpose here was to maintain his investment and develop his reporting skills. By recording the shared lesson, it provided him a specific role on how he could take part in a whole group lesson and gave him a purpose. The recording activity also supported his skills in staying regulated, focused, and invested. The positive impact was immediate. He was meaningfully included, and we were able to use his recordings and post them in our electronic classroom (e.g., Google, Canvas, etc.). By posting the videos, we provided peers that may have been absent that day an access point as well as other classmates—including himself—to refer back to as needed to reteach, redirect, or to reinforce the expectations for learning. An incidental benefit that we also discovered was how we could use these recordings to address social norms or cues taking place that we might have missed during the live instruc-

tion. The return on investment was invaluable at this point for all of us.

"*What might I consider trying to enhance learners' investment?*"

As you read on, you'll see more of how Kevin's passion grew throughout the unit, how it was nurtured, and the ways we utilized it throughout the "3i's" of engagement. There are many ways to approach thinking differently when planning and designing learning opportunities. Consider how we grow and enjoy plants. Let's use this analogy of plants to consider how we design learning experiences. When growing a plant from seed, we first fertilize the soil, then we provide sunshine and water, and finally we harvest and enjoy the final product. What if we apply this plant growing process to our lesson plan designs?

Fertilize the Soil

Before the unit, consider opportunities that will be encouraged throughout the learning:

- Create investment by gathering interest in the learning topics;
- Design supports to promote independence for learners to access, use, and generate fluency in the learning; and
- Provide opportunities for learners to identify how they want to share what they know with others in a variety of ways to show initiation.

Provide Sunshine and Water

During the unit this is the learning. Similar to providing sunshine and water to a plant, we:

- Provide information in consistent and familiar ways;
- Give variety in the options for content engagement to ensure purpose and motivation and enhance the learning experiences; and
- Create and value options for how they demonstrate and share their knowledge and skills.

Harvest and Enjoy

At the end of the unit, we share and celebrate the learning. This is equally as important as all the preparation and content learning. The harvest is a time to:

- Notice others learning;
- Hear about their experiences;
- Share our own learning with one another;
- Gather ideas for future learning experiences; and
- Generate excitement around learning and as a learning community.

When we outline a lesson or design a unit in a similar way as to growing a plant, it gives us the structure to think differently. Here's what this might look like when you take action to design with the "3i's" of engagement in mind while you fertilize the soil, provide sunshine and water, and harvest and enjoy the full processes of learning.

ınvestment

Before the Unit: Fertilize the Soil

Offer learners a survey to see what their interests are around the topic.

- Prior to taking the survey, have learners manipulate and preview various materials and resources that represented the various content topics (such as videos, books, articles, etc.)

- Spend time as a class getting excited, reacting, and learning more about...

  ○ How an informational text is written and organized

  ○ How authors grab attention

  ○ Commonalities that we noticed authors using

Side note: this would serve as a basis for our writing and build our awareness of our learning

The data gathered will

- Support intentionality in connecting peers with common interests

- Guide the educator to prepare and curate materials

- Provide access to resources that are relevant and appropriate based on interests

A learner survey before the unit also provides

- A preview to what's coming next creating predictability

- Gives learners the opportunity to share their voice

- Learners will have their interests considered and connected to the content

- Skills as expert learners who are purposeful and motivated are reinforced

During the Unit: Provide Sunshine and Water

Ask learners to generate relevant questions to guide exploration and growth so they can dig in.
 	
Create anchor charts to capture and inspire new learning around the various topics.
    Why? This provided a way for learners to engage in new learning and to share learning based on a collective group of reactions the group(s) are having to the topic, to the reading and with the research we are doing.
 	
Share, connect, and monitor growth and progress.
    Why? Being purposeful in learning through self-reflection shows how we were growing as experts within the chosen topic (e.g., weather).
 	
In self-reflection, we spend time on developing and analyzing questions, along with monitoring and assessing resources used and hearing other's "aha" findings.
    Why? To support our expert learner skills in motivation. Others' excitement may generate my own excitement in the learning topic (e.g., weather).

End of Unit: Harvest and Enjoy
Connect with the learners on why this learning topic relates to real life and explore choices on why engagement in a showcase or gallery to share products of their learning is valuable. Offer the opportunity to reflect on "Why might this apply to other areas in my life?" and maybe, "Why was learning about this important to me?" Harvest and Share Idea: Create a *Gallery Walk* as a way to showcase learning products and see others' work as if you're walking through a museum, taking in all the collections on display.
SEL Connection: Self Awareness
Self-awareness skills by fostering self-efficacy to recognize strengths and areas of interest.

If you have an interest to learn more about ways to support learner investment, I encourage you to explore some of the authors mentioned in the references, as there is a lot of stellar work in our field that gives us ideas to consider.

independence

Independence is the WHAT of engagement. Our resourcefulness. It is the learning fluency that provides access for engagement in learning.

When we consider independence, we are fostering opportunities during solo as well as social scenarios. To do this, we need to focus on the learners' access to information being presented in different ways, using modeling, clarity of expectations, graphics, photos, or multiple media options and also ensuring there are peer models within close proximity to one another's learning experiences.

To support fostering independence and finding value in clarifying information, consider:

- Pairing language with an opportunity for learners to connect what is being discussed to personal and real-life experiences.

- Providing opportunities for learners to follow or create visuals such as written "to do" lists, task organizers, time chunking, or schedules to support transitions within and across activities or projects.

- Opportunities to observe modeling or examples provided by others in real-time or via recordings of academic and social expectations.

- Clarification of social expectations such as volume level, energy level and physical proximity to others in both familiar and unfamiliar situations.

- Options for learners to use or make visuals or written reminders to clarify conversation expectations such as which topics to choose, when to talk, and when to wait or listen.

- Self-reflect opportunities on one's own actions in relation to social expectations and follow or create supports for future settings.

Let's check in to show how Kevin is doing.

Kevin, along with his peers, has been invested in the learning experience. There is a buzz of energy in our classroom about being meteorologist experts. As learners continue to be motivated and show investment in their learning, we, as educators, are observing and noticing how they are independently approaching the experiences. We notice this by their navigating of the expectations and fluency within the routines. Their academic growth and progress in the content areas show us this evidence too. Incidentally, we also notice their investment socially as they engage in collaborative groups. We recognize and believe that learning is personal, yet social. We know that independence is critical to engagement. Specifically, Kevin was observed to dig into his own research, resources, and thinking. He independently navigated resources that we prepared for learners to use, such as the textbooks and video interviews. We even are starting to see him seek out opportunities in our day to share with peers. As his educators, we recognized that Kevin was falling in love with the social world like never before.

"What am I already doing to ensure learners' independence?"

This was our opportunity to notice how we support Kevin in a meaningful way to enhance his independence. We continuously ask ourselves, "Are we intentionally designing and embedding supports for when and how to engage in the content and with others?" We asked ourselves, "Are supports consistently in our routines?" and "Were the social expectations presented in multiple ways and accessible?" We specifically focused on the times when it was socially expected to share, talk, and process with those around him. We took these opportunities of excitement and joy to help bring awareness to social cues and "how am I, how are we" learning.

We considered the various components within our classroom when learners were asked to demonstrate learning Independently, in a partnership, small group, or whole group. We clarified what the expectations were for navigating materials, voice volume, tone, and peer turn taking. With Kevin in our class, we had the opportunity to recognize that all learners benefit from these reminders and supports, so it became something we did universally. We just did it.

We provided visual support that helped reinforce the transitions that occurred throughout the lesson for the class. We created anchor charts and bookmarks with sentence starters. We put labels on just about everything, and set up rules that gave learners permission to get what they believed they needed to engage in their learning. We even had a space for where to go and stand if you didn't know what you needed, but you knew you might need something to help you do your best learning. This built awareness and reinforcement of expectations on how to independently learn, engage, and make sure that we, as educators, were supporting all learners in reaching the personal and social goals that we had set and established.

But what about the content area goals and progress? As mentioned earlier, Kevin had a passion for camera work and recording. Therefore, our question for exploration became how we could find a relevant, real-life example of how meteorology (content) and reporting connect? And furthermore, how would this connect to content standards? This led us to the idea of weathermen and news reporting, considering how they gather information and think of ways to inform and share it with their viewers. This became not only a way to sustain his investment, but also a way to build independence as he immersed himself in various ways to learn more about weather, about reporting, and about consumers of information.

Through learning from experts as he watched news forecasts

and news anchors describing weather events, to learning how to present information from reviewing expert models and interviewing other peer "experts" working on a similar topic or actually interviewing field experts, Kevin has developed the skills of conversation by asking questions, listening, and acquiring information. He has even indirectly developed his skill of turn-taking. He is working on organizing information using a graphic organizer. He shows us his content learning by reading and manipulating informational text, drawing on text features to support his final product. We are seeing his engagement increase, and are thrilled to see him be independently engaged in his learning.

"What might I consider trying to enhance learners' independence?"

Let's continue in our lesson or design of a unit as if we are growing a plant. This analogy gives us the structures to think differently. Here's what this might look like when with a focus on independence as you take action to fertilize the soil, provide sunshine and water, and harvest and en- joy the full processes of learning.

independence

UDL Guidelines and the "3i's" of Engagement
The WHAT of Learning & Learner Independence

Before the Unit: Fertilize the Soil

Intentionally design of the learner output based on common and personal goals.

- Educators pre-select relevant and useful resources and have a form (system) prepared for when learners desire a different resource that is relevant and useful.

- Encourage flexibility to choose and learn from resources, including—but not limited to—hard copy books, e-texts, websites, videos, and experts they could talk to.

- Provided insight for what they already know about each of the topics through creative opportunities to pull out prior knowledge.

  - Ideas might be

    - Graffiti anchor charts

    - "Would you rather?" questions

    - "Did you know?" facts that connect to the topics

Side note: By modeling creative ways to think about topics, we set learners up to be creative in their own thinking. This creativity may guide their topic research, give insights to keywords, or get the juices flowing to generate other ideas.

Use the learner surveys to group based on their interests and consider the benefits of both homogeneous and heterogeneous grouping.

- Connect peers with common interests

Side note: In the example at this point in the learning, there were more benefits of homogeneous groupings to gather information related to similar topics of interest.

- Support learners to select materials that connect to their topic of interest.

- Guide learners to use a variety of resources that have been pre-pulled for them.

Side note: Learners who tend to use one type of resource or reference modality may benefit from having a visual support that will enhance the likelihood that they will use multiple resources. A tic-tac-toe board to make three in a row for using a variety of resources could be one way to encourage variety.

Create learning fluency.

- Employ the structure and routine of peer partnerships or core groups

- Provide partner suggestions with both similar and different interests to ask questions, process information and discuss possible areas for adjustment

During the Unit: Provide Sunshine and Water

Get creative in the learning to generate ideas and give learners the space to be resourceful in what they use to guide their experiences.

Gather information about their knowledge and resourcefulness by

- Conducting an informational writing pre-assessment to indicate where the writers were upon entering the unit to encourage use of resources that will support independence throughout the writing process.

- Providing multiple options of learner-friendly rubrics to capture information from oneself, educators, and peers.

- Encourage the use of rubric feedback on writing to adjust goals and to enhance process and development in their topics.

Present information in different ways by

- Explore opportunities within a mini lesson to offer an expert model as well as peer models to see how their peers are thinking or processing information.

- Create independence by having key structures and templates in place that support anchored conversations and social expectations; this will create accountability and give responsibility to an individual and as a group, when feasible.

- Sharing reading and writing lectures in a spiraled and interconnected way. *Side note: A spiraled approach supports all learners through repetition as well as access to the learning through repetition in different ways and at different times within the unit.*

Model ways to consider information and share a variety of ways to organize thoughts by

- Demonstrating "think-alouds;" this is similar to "read-alouds," but without the text.

- Modeling ways to organize thoughts into notes and text structures.

- Show learners what to note and where to put it in a thinking or graphic organizer.

- Noticing in text structures authors use and which ones we might use or pull into our information writing.

- Sharing prior learner examples to demonstrate thought processes and opportunities to clarify information such as vocabulary or literacy structures.

Provide optional times for learners to gather more information or direct instruction by

- Offering instructional invitations to learners to attend an additional seminar.

- Directly modeling ways to use various text structures.
- Highlighting big ideas, author and writer patterns or other critical features noticed.

End of Unit: Harvest and Share

Connect with the learners on what about this learning experience enhances their skills with resource management and their overall growth in their knowledge of the content and social experiences.

Provide the opportunity to interact and learn from their peers' final product, specifically what they choose to do and what was shared with others about their learning.

- After hearing others share, have learners write down reactions:
  - "What gave them an idea?"
  - "What did they connect with?"
  - "What did they learn?"
  - "What was exciting about it?"
- Highlight ideas by bringing these responses back to the purpose of why there is a need for multiple resources and text to learn about a topic.

Offer the opportunity to reflect on "What worked for me to be independent?" and "What might enhance or improve my independence?" and maybe, "What will I do differently next time?"

Harvest and Share Idea:
  Write, edit, illustrate an article about a topic studied for a class-wide news magazine to showcase learners' stories, their art, or their graphic designs, and publish it to share with the class and their communities.

SEL Connection: Responsible Decision Making, Self-Awareness and Self-Management

Responsible decision making, self-awareness and self-management skills are addressed by developing communication, social engagement, relationship building and teamwork as well as goal setting and organization skills. By identifying one's emotions, recognizing strengths and self-efficacy to persevere when you get frustrated and managing oneself to successfully regulate, to notice impulsivity and identify opportunities to stay on topic and opportunities to demonstrate self-discipline when having access to multiple resources.

In order to enhance independence and provide learners with these opportunities, educators can create a higher likelihood of success by embedding consistent routines into our learning structures, and when we provide a variety of resources for social expectations. So, let's take a moment to reflect. Do you remember a classroom routine from your school days? How did that classroom routine guide you as a learner? Now, consider what classroom routines you currently have in place.

> Name the routine:
>   Posting a recording of a lesson component in a shared electronic space.
>
> What's the purpose?
>   For learners to review at a later time.
>   To provide an opportunity for learners to press pause or rewind when needed.
>
> How does it enhance learning fluency and independence, not compliance?
>   Learners can access the posted material, review it at their own pace and with ease, and demonstrate their expert learning abilities in being resourceful and knowledgeable.

After reading this educator's perspective, think of your own experiences or teaching practices that enhance independence within the learning experience.

> Name the routine:
>
> What's the purpose?
>
> How does it enhance learning fluency, not compliance?

To learn more about ways to support learner independence and to review resources that will enhance learning independence, I encourage you to explore some of the authors mentioned in the references, as there are a plethora of tools, materials, and resources that may spark ideas.

initiation

Initiation is the HOW of engagement. Our actions to share information with others. It is the expression that provides a desire for engagement in learning.

The opportunity to enhance initiation for learners can also be an area of focus as it is another essential skill in the "3i's" of engagement. In order to foster initiation, learners who have varying options to show what they know and have frequent opportunities to initiate in everyday activities that vary in social complexity will enhance the skills related to initiation.

To foster opportunities for learner initiation through expression and communication, consider:

- Creating opportunities for learners to use or develop replica sets of visual supports and written language for use during interactions.

- Incorporating opportunities for learners to use or design visual supports for content (i.e., what to say), timing (i.e., when to talk), and socialization (i.e., how to engage).

- Providing opportunities for learners to use or create multiple options for expression (e.g., a selection of sentences to point to or hold, a dry erase board, hand gestures like thumbs up or thumbs down, communication switches with recorded comments, sharing with a peer).

- Balancing adult and peer interactions with frequent opportunities for learners to both follow and lead interactions by honoring invitations and embedding opportunities.

- Creating frequent collaboration opportunities with others (e.g., turn and talk, group collaboration, taking on roles within interactions).

- Universally provide visual sentence starters or phrases for what to say (e.g., "I am thinking…," "I notice that…," "I heard you say…," or "That makes me think…").

- Providing close proximity and continuous access to visuals such as graphics and written language (e.g., sentence starters, cue cards, reminders of what to say).

Let's check in again on Kevin.

"What am I already doing to ensure learners' initiations?"

Kevin, along with his peers, has neared the end of the unit. Therefore, as readers, writers, and scientists, it was time for us to start thinking about how to formally share out and celebrate our new learning and expertise. Within this unit, we focused on developing ourselves as readers and writers of informational text using weather as the vehicle. The purpose behind this type of reading and writing was to learn and acquire new information and to inform. Our opportunity was in how our learners chose to do this. Together, we scaffolded when needed; ultimately, the learners determined what will be. As educators, our role is to recognize the different options and ways for learners to express and take action on the learning acquired.

So, how did Kevin do this? He showed passion, strategy, and drive throughout this learning. He shared his learning and journey as a news reporter and weatherman through a private "TV channel and network." His informational writing piece became the script for his weather report. This writing piece was crafted by the information he gained through the learning opportunities and was released by hearing Kevin read aloud his informational texts on the weather topic he chose. As he read, dictated, wrote, and shared his learning, he was given time, space, and the opportunity to grow and learn alongside his peers in both academic and social ways. Prior to this, opportunities like these were not typically available to learners like Kevin. We could see that learning is social, yet personal for Kevin and his peers. We now know that social connections "fuel the brain to grow." We had Kevin to thank as he showed us this every day. Kevin emphasized the value each learner brings to our community when they show what they know. Throughout this unit, in our planning, we dug in to proactively design with all learners in mind. It was messy. It was challenging. It was hard. Yet, it was also thrilling, exciting, and so worth it because with challenge comes opportunity. The opportunity for us was to think differently and appreciate what works.

"What might I consider trying to enhance learners' initiations?"

ịnitiation

UDL Guidelines and the "3i's" of Engagement
The HOW of Learning & Learner Initiation

Before the Unit: Fertilize the Soil

Consider the executive functioning, planning, or organizational skills of learners. This may include how learners organize information and plan to share their learning.

- Think about timelines and tasks in how the unit will be developed and shared with the learners.

- Consider how to provide various opportunities for learners to share their learning with one another.

- Consider whether providing options for the learning composition or construction of projects would be feasible; if so, develop scaffolded supports and rubrics to guide learners.

During the Unit: Provide Sunshine and Water

Provide opportunities for learners to initiate and notice how others initiate by

- Using rubrics, routine checks, and guides along the way to ensure learners are feeling supported and confident about their learning, direction, and progress.

- Providing learners options to gather information strategically in order to learn more about their topic through multiple resources that represent similar information.

- Showing learners how videos or multimedia sources share and develop information for their audience.

Side note: Part of this process encourages the skills of paying attention to not only what we learned and how we grew our expertise, but also how the author or writer communicated to you their audience to share information.

Guide learners in their planning, strategies, and goal-setting.

- As learners develop their informational writing pieces, provide organization options which may include

  - ○ Graphic organizers
  - ○ Whiteboard note-taking
  - ○ Questions to ask myself
  - ○ Slidedeck templates
  - ○ Fill-in the blanks
  - ○ Movie script template
  - ○ Any other way that may guide the transfer, generalization, and organization of their thinking for the purpose of sharing it effectively and efficiently with others.

- Have learners continue to self-evaluate, give, and receive feedback about their particular growth and learning within the content to show they are comprehending and attaining goals that have been set personally, socially, as well as academically.

Offer opportunities for learners to be strategic in how they engage in this learning.

- Give feedback in a variety of ways.

- Consider varying from having a conversation to give input through notation directly on a copy of the learner's work.

- Give structures for peer-to-peer generated input.

Side note: Using a variety of informal and formal feedback methods supports learners to hear and respond to the input given by others.

End of Unit: Harvest and Share

Connect with the learners on how this learning enhanced their initiation skills.

Sharing information to show what you know and the overall growth in knowledge.

- Identify how learners felt comfortable and confident in the learning. Specifically, when they feel like they were in their learning zone versus the panic or comfort zones based on how they were engaged in the learning.

- Offer ways to share and enjoy our own as well as others learning that is purposeful and meaningful to them.

Provide the opportunity to interact and learn from their peers. Specifically, how they choose to engage in their learning and share it with others.

- Provide opportunities for learners to discuss the connections to
  - Real-life application
  - Personal experiences
  - Other content learning

- Offer the opportunity to reflect on
  - "How might this apply to other areas in my life?"
  - "How did I meet or adjust my goal?"
  - "How did I grow as a learner specifically in the management of resources, monitoring progress, planning, or strategy development?"

SEL Connection: Social Awareness, Relationship Skill, and Responsible Decision-Making

Social awareness, relationship skills, and responsible decision-making skills are addressed by developing communication through repeated learning opportunities with others. Through social engagement with peers and educators to gain input and feedback; through building or expanding organizational skills by observing others or using various resources; though developing relationships by accepting perspectives who have similar as well as different interests or opinions; and through goals by managing, adjusting, or setting new ones.

Do you know a "Kevin"? Do you recognize and notice what works and design learning experiences with these "3i's" of engagement in mind?

How might designing plans with the "3'is" of engagement in mind value you as the educator?

How might it enhance what you value in learners?

To explore more about ways to enhance opportunities for learner initiation and for additional resources to support varying levels of a learner, consider exploring some of the authors mentioned in the references.

FOUR

RESOURCES FOR GROWTH

What Enhances Learner Engagement

An opportunity to self-reflect

It is valuable to have data in order to assess learning. It is also extremely important to use the data in a useful manner. In this section you will have an opportunity to reflect and appreciate yourself. It is my hope that you discover an opportunity to engage in your own learning in a meaningful way. The collective impact is low when professional development is done in isolation and there is a disconnect between what we learn versus what we apply in our practice. According to the research of Joyce and Showers (1981), "Most professional development results in less than 10 percent transfer into practice." My hope is that this self-reflection tool supports you to realize that the status quo is a no-go. Below are some statements to support you in discovering your future opportunities to think differently.

SCALE FOR SELF-REFLECTION

🪴	**I don't know yet,** and I hope to learn more about learner engagement.
🌱	I am **slightly knowledgeable** about learner engagement, and I **rarely or am not yet** using this information to inform my practice with learners.
🌿	I am **somewhat knowledgeable** about learner engagement, and I **occasionally and inconsistently** use this information to inform my practice with learners.

	I am **knowledgeable** about learner engagement, and I **usually and frequently** use this information to inform my practice with learners.
	I am **confident in my knowledge** of learner engagement, and I **constantly and continually** use this information to inform my practice with learners.

Self-Reflection: Use the boxes below the plant pots to shade in your responses. You may be between a few—and that's okay, just shade them in accordingly.

1. I believe that enhancing learners' **investment** and supporting their sustained engagement is important.
 	
I know this to be true because,
    I can recognize when my learners are invested, and able to sustain that investment, in a natural activity or lesson.
 	
    I plan and include learner interests as a means to stimulate investment and motivation and provide support for sustaining this engagement in developmentally appropriate ways.	

2. I believe that enhancing learners' **independence** and adherence to social norms and fluency within routines is important.
 	
I know this to be true because,
    I can recognize when my learners are independent and adhering to everyday routines, social norms, and expectations in natural activities or lessons.
 	
    I plan and include examples, visuals, role models and tools that they can access to enhance independence in developmentally appropriate ways.	

THINK DIFFERENTLY

3. I believe that enhancing learners' **initiation** by providing different options and opportunities for sharing and expressing is important.

I know this to be true because,
> I can recognize when my learners are initiating, and able to show what they know (nonverbally or verbally), in a natural activity or lesson.

> I plan and include a range of options for my learners to initiate by responding to both nonverbal and verbal forms of expression and providing many opportunities for communication.

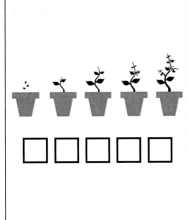

Notes to myself:

The information you shared in this self-reflection will be useful in the next section. It will guide you in this journey to enrich, grow, and nurture yourself. Remember, this work is all part of a larger process that encourages and supports us to think differently.

Supports to guide you

Make the choice in what you do next based on your responses in the self-reflection. There are a collection of ideas in the forthcoming sections and additional ones in other places and spaces of your life. These next few sections provide a variety of ideas that can be a useful guide for where you choose to go. You will notice there are multiple images for each of the following opportunities (enrich, grow, nurture) because learning is messy and an inexact science. Dig in, get dirty, and think differently.

Consider the "3i's" of engagement (investment, independence, and initiation) to complete the following statements.

I believe ("3i" of engagement) _____ is (adjective) _____.

I can:

I plan to and will include:

After the plant grows a bit, I'm curious... has anything else sprouted or wilted?

ENRICH

If you answered with the first two images in the self-reflection, you have the opportunity to further *enrich* yourself. What does it mean to enrich? In this context, we will reference enrich as an opportunity to dig into your learning with a focus on learner engagement. Through reading, observing, and exploring resources, there may be a direct impact on your approach to engaging everyone in the learning experiences.

When considering **your** enrichment opportunities, it is critical to explore a variety of nutrients and the nutritive value of what they might bring to your practices. Similar to growing a plant, it is beneficial to consider the amount of sunlight, water, air quality, and nutrients in the soil to enrich the soil for a plant's growth. Reflecting on yourself in this way could be an opportunity for you to use your "livewired" brain to consider a different way of thinking. You could learn more about how predictability in daily lessons and fostering learners' self-regulation is valuable. You could work to design lessons through strategic planning and implementation of developmentally appropriate accommodations. Maybe you will focus on ways to enhance learners' engagement. Considering how you can modify or provide options within lessons to include materials of high learner interest is equally as important as the rigor of the content and the pace of delivery. There are various opportunities for how to *enrich* ourselves here.

Let's dig into the "3i's" of engagement to *enrich* our knowledge and skills.

 Enhance learner's *investment* and supporting their effort and persistence through the use of self-regulation skills and strategies. When learners are motivated and able to sustain investment in an activity, lesson, or experience, they are engaged in learning.

To enrich *investment* within learning experiences, I can:

- Get the hook by piquing the learners' interests in a brief amount of time. As the facilitator of learning, this can be done by creating curiosity through actions, material presentations, or both.
  - The hook might be
    - A mystery box of "things" that are connected to the content
    - An educator dressed up as a character
    - An auditory resource like a video, song, lyric, poem, etc.
    - A series of footprints on the floor with clues which creates anticipation
- Providing choices to learners will peak motivation. As the facilitator of learning, you can encourage choice through actions, varying material presentation, or both.
  - The choices might be
    - Appealing to sensory qualities
    - Opportunities to use hands-on materials
    - Connected to real-life application
    - Embedding learner's interests into the experiences

- Discovering what motivates learners by conducting an interest survey

- Developing the support for learners to find relevance and freedom in their learning. As the facilitator of learning, you can be an active model of interpersonal and learning support through your actions, presentation of materials, or both.

  - The interpersonal and learning supports may include

    - Tools to stay actively engaged (e.g., fidgets, drawing utensils, sketchpad)

    - Supports to persist in tasks that engage positive regulation strategies such as self-talk, affirmation, intrinsic motivation reminders, etc.

    - Reminders or visuals for ways to regulate emotions

    - Reassurance from others if or when learners become distressed

    - Peers and adults who are responsive and interactive partners

 When we provide support that promotes *independence*, it guides learners through routines and social norms. Learners access these role models, tools, visuals, and other environmental supports to enhance predictability that promote independence.

To enrich *independence* within learning experiences, I can:

Incorporate predictability within my learning environment and in the materials. As the facilitator of learning, I can provide options for learners to see, hear and perceive information in a variety of ways that will promote independence through predictability.

Actions that encourage independence may include:

- Creating routines in the classroom
- Following a daily or task schedule

- Using routines within lesson plans
- Making visual learning tools
- Develop visual lists such as checklists, "to do" lists, tic-tac-toe task boards, etc.
- Providing role models or videos of expectations or desired outcomes
- Having materials accessible throughout all learning opportunities

Provide access to information by presenting it in different ways. As the facilitator of learning, I can provide opportunities for learners to experience information through various modalities.

Ideas that give learners access to information may be presented in a variety of ways:

- Present information through visual, auditory, or tactile modes
- Adjust the visual layout of information to include text features such as larger fonts, bolded or italic text, headings, color-coding, etc.
- Use technology, digital media, or other electronic resources to represent content
- Consistency of symbols, icons, and color schemes create familiarity and predictability
- Customize information to add captions, graphics, text boxes, highlighting, etc.

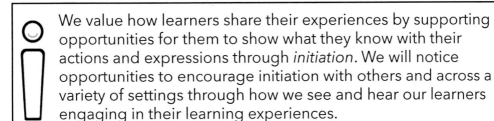

We value how learners share their experiences by supporting opportunities for them to show what they know with their actions and expressions through *initiation*. We will notice opportunities to encourage initiation with others and across a variety of settings through how we see and hear our learners engaging in their learning experiences.

To enrich *initiations* within learning experiences, I can...

Provide options for how learners interact in the lesson content and social experiences. As the facilitator of learning, I can create options for how learners will share or interact with the learning to express what they know.

I can provide learners options to demonstrate their learning by:

- Encouraging a variety of output modalities to express learning such as recording themselves, playing games, creating a demonstration, etc.

- Accepting and promoting learning that looks different yet shows the content

- Prompting learners to use various curricular materials to demonstrate learning, such as connecting a math concept to a literacy project

Providing experiences to express their learning with others:

- Adjusting the social experiences to interact with peers by providing sentence starters, or example phrases for learners to express

- Creating a balance in the instruction for learners to lead as well as follow along in the learning experiences

- Develop cue cards with assigned roles and responsibilities for group members when doing small group activities or projects

- Co-creating with the learner tools such as a bookmark with phrases that can be used in a small group or peer learning experience

- Provide predictable peer partners and groupings to build trust and flow within peer learning experiences

The powerful influence of interest on learner motivation is captured by Xiang et al. (2005), who reported that interest "emerged as the most important intrinsic motivation construct for predicting future intention..." (p. 193). You are the expert learner here who chooses what's working as you design what's next in your journey. Based on the ideas shared in this section, consider discovering some things you're doing or ideas you want to do. I encourage you to incorporate some of these into your educational practices. Thank you for taking the time to complete the self-reflection to embrace an opportunity to enrich yourself.

I will *enrich* experiences by:

GROW

Given your responses in this self-reflection, you may choose to explore growth opportunities specific to the "3i's" of engagement. This growth moment means you feel nourished, and this is an opportunity to grow your knowledge and skills.

One area to consider is the predictability of the learning environment. The rules and routines in our lives eventually form into habits. These newly formed habits allow our neurological systems to relax and engage with the new information being provided. When we know how a specific individual learns best, we can put accommodations in place that support that learner's ability to predict and habitualize these rules and routines. When we do this, we create an atmosphere for "learning fluency." A learner's anxiety can be reduced and engagement can be increased through the provision of predictable learning environments.

Consider an opportunity to grow your awareness of a learner's perspective by thinking about these prediction prompts. Dig into how information is set up for learners. When we respond "yes" or identify a "no," then we have more information to consider and support our entry point for growth. Maybe we ask a learner to answer a prompt of "how do you predict...?" we gain insights into how they see their learning spaces. Our opportunity is to grow our knowledge and skills with the "3i's" of engagement to enhance ourselves as educators and promote learner success and fluency within their learning.

The learner can...	Y	N
Predict that others are a source of assistance		
Predict that others are a source of engagement or pleasure		
Predict the sequence of activities/tasks		
Predict the steps within each activity/task		
Predict what to say		
Predict how to engage in the activity/task		
Predict how to regulate emotions with respect for self and others		
Predict the purpose of academic and social activities/tasks		

Another area to consider is persistence and sustained effort. When learning occurs within a person's zone of proximal development, the amount of time, effort, and persistence will increase. Psychologist Mihaly Csíkszentmihályi's (2014) seminal work, *Flow: The Psychology of Optimal Experience*, is worth noting specifically when speaking to the potential of student engagement. Csíkszentmihályi theorized that people are most happy in a state of flow, which he defined as "complete absorption" with the activity and situation in which they are engaged. Sometimes learners will say they are "in a flow" when they are moving through a task with ease, seemingly losing track of time. We can have more opportunities to make meaningful connections to prior knowledge, experiences and learning when we understand a learner's interests. When we do this, when we truly believe in all learners' abilities to learn, we can create a "fireworks show" in their brains, connecting synapses and creating truly engaging experiences within universally accessible learning environments. The time we take for ourselves to grow is endlessly valuable; I hope you find this to be true.

> Enhancing learner's *investment* and supporting their effort and persistence through the use of self-regulation skills and strategies. When learners are motivated and able to sustain investment in an activity, lesson, or experience, they are engaged in learning.

To grow *investment* within learning experiences, I can:

- Support learners to develop goals to sustain effort and persistence in learning
- Give feedback about learner effort levels and personal growth within a timely manner
- Create a balance of the demands being placed on the learner
- Provide a range of resources to the learner that are readily available for when the learner feels they are useful
- Develop opportunities to collaborate with peers, professionals, other educators, etc.
- Generate direct input for the learners to use and adjust from
- Vary the level of difficulty in learning experiences, roles, and responsibilities

> When we provide support that promotes *independence*, it guides learners through routines and social norms. Learners' access these role models, tools, visuals, and other environmental supports to enhance predictability that promote independence.

To grow *independence* within learning experiences, I can:

- Develop resources that support clarity of language and course-specific vocabulary
- Incorporate visual supports to support learner understanding of concepts
- Use and provide access to manipulatives or hands-on learning materials

- Provide cue cards, formula index cards, or other resources that provide support and pre-teach essential terms

- Use consistent design templates or images and visuals to generate predictability, thus enhancing the understanding of displayed information

- Incorporate multimedia to combine visuals, text, audio, and graphics

- Make connections across learned concepts, ideas, subjects, and learner interests

> We value how learners share their experiences by supporting opportunities for them to show what they know with their actions and expressions through *initiation*. We will notice opportunities to encourage initiation with others and across a variety of settings through how we see and hear our learners engaging in their learning experiences.

To grow *initiations* within learning experiences, I can...

- Provide learners with choices in how to demonstrate their learning to show what they know

- Model and encourage collaboration with peers to generate a product that shows learning

- Provide continuous access to manipulatives or hands-on learning materials to support learner output of knowledge

- Create scaffolded opportunities to guide learner performance and learning products

- Provide a variety of options to learners such as practicing a skill using an app or peer re-teaching of a skill or concept

- Opportunities to perform or act-out what the learner knows lifting it off the paper and putting into action for others to see and experience

As we explore opportunities to incorporate some of these ideas intentionally into our planning we can also consider engaging in a mentorship with a colleague that will support us to notice what's working and grow in our practices. A way to do this might be peer-to-peer learning. Learn and grow from one another by observing and collaborating using an appreciative inquiry process. Consider selecting one of the "3i's" of engagement to explore and dig into a bit deeper. Provide yourself with the evidence that shares how learner engagement increases when we consider and design for their investment, independence, and initiation throughout the learning.

I will experience growth by:

NURTURE

Based on your responses in the self-reflection, you may benefit from nurturing experiences that are specific to learner engagement. You may also wish to explore how to create opportunities to appreciate yourself as a practitioner. Your enrichment and growth in the idea that all styles of learners engage in meaningful learning experiences drive what you do as an educator and your knowledge in teaching practices has landed you here. Now, it is time to nurture yourself with some resources designed to take your skills to the next level.

As you read about this nurture opportunity, think about how you can further connect your knowledge with your practices. In an interview conducted by Dunleavy and Milton (2009), the participating students stated that engaging learning includes considering teacher's ideas and having opportunities to "see how subjects are interconnected, learn from and with each other and other people in their community, and have more opportunities for dialogue and conversations" (p. 10). For example, as you think about your planning practice, ask yourself if you reference or use a learner profile. This could be something that has been completed by the learner, with a learner, or on behalf of the learner. Here are some ideas that can enhance the "3i's" of engagement as you intentionally design learning experiences.

 Enhance learners' *investment* and supporting their effort and persistence through the use of self-regulation skills and strategies. When learners are motivated and able to sustain investment in an activity, lesson, or experience, they are engaged in learning.

To nurture *investment* within learning experiences, I can:

- Provide options to set goals and self-regulate

- Understand what motivates learners and promote learners to incorporate this into their learning experiences

- Establish a base understanding of learner beliefs about the content or areas of study

- Demonstrate strategies for regulation and embed these opportunities across all learning experiences and within the learning environments

- Create and encourage feedback loops that provide opportunities for reflection

 When we provide support that promotes *independence*, it guides learners through routines and social norms. Learners access these role models, tools, visuals, and other environmental supports to enhance predictability that promote independence.

To nurture *independence* within learning experiences, I can:

- Provide options to make sense and understand knowledgeUse pri-

THINK DIFFERENTLY

or experiences and connections to background knowledge

- Showcase patterns or highlight critical information and ideas
- Provide cues or visual aides to support the learner to identify extraneous parts
- Be a guide for learners to process information and make strong connections across content areas, environments, and within personal life experiences
- Encourage strategies that learners can make their knowledge applicable in their experiences

We value how learners share their experiences by supporting opportunities for them to show what they know with their actions and expressions through *initiation*. We will notice opportunities to encourage initiation with others and across a variety of settings through how we see and hear our learners engaging in their experiences.

To nurture *initiations* within learning experiences, I can provide options to plan, strategize, and initiate action by...

- Creating opportunities for learners to set goals
- Discovering the skills that learners may need to learn or have guided instruction to support their skill development
- Guiding learners in their goals and encourage them to be attainable, yet challenging
- Modeling and support implementation of learning strategies to get the most of our experiences
- Having supports in place to aid learners in their "pause and reflect" moments
- Being a facilitator of learning opportunities by providing resources and modeling strategies
- Honoring the learners' working memory
- Giving timely feedback to support goals and the implementation of strategies

Now, let's shift from the perspective of our planning and designing for learners to the nurturing of ourselves. Good teaching involves self-reflection, but have you considered recording yourself and watching your footage with a reflective, appreciative lens? Turning the lens on yourself may be uncomfortable, but it can help you to gain deep insight into areas where you are successful. It also provides you with real-life, relevant, and timely resources to share with others, and may even show you small opportunities for nurturing yourself in your own implementation of practices.

Consider looking for learning strategies, some of which are noted above, that enable learners to predict the sequence of activities and the steps towards task completion. Or, look for ways learners in which use self-regulation strategies to maintain the optimal level of arousal for the learning environment, task, or activity. These strategies foster a learner's sustained effort and persistence. When we model these strategies of self-regulation for our learners, we are all nurtured. Consider how you nurture these skills in learners through deliberate instruction or modeling as you watch your footage. Also, think about how you implement options for recruiting learner interests as a means to stimulate and motivate them in their learning. I'm confident you have what you need, and all you have to do now is appreciate yourself and notice it.

Another opportunity to nurture yourself is peer-to-peer feedback. The consistent implementation of learning strategies that enable learners to predict the sequence of activities and the steps toward completion can be powerful ways to support them in their development of becoming expert learners and promotes their engagement in learning. Nurture yourself to understand and explain how you consistently implement developmentally appropriate strategies, paired with accommodations, to foster learners' purpose and motivation. Their use of resources and knowledge in how they are strategic and goal-directed across learning experiences is important to recognize. Discovering strong ways to ensure authentic learner engagement and motivation to learn comes from consistent planning, designing, and implementation. As you nurture

THINK DIFFERENTLY

your own skills, it is critical to recognize that others can now learn from you. What motivates or inspires you? What are you passionate about? How can you find those answers for yourself while partnering with others to encourage them too? I encourage you to make a partnership with a colleague. Nurture yourself, and make time to be appreciated.

> I will explore nurture opportunities by:

So, what's next?

It is critical to realize that you may be in many areas of learning at the same time when it comes to these "3i's" of engagement. I encourage you to embrace this reality, as well as to explore each area as it makes sense to you and your purpose for reading this book. At times, you might find yourself in an enrichment arena for independence or a nurture experience for investment. This is natural, and you can expect it to be true for you. The goal is to enrich, grow, and nurture yourself throughout the process, and I invite you to keep reading to learn more about how to do so. I hope you choose to join me in Part III, where we get curious and continue to value ourselves in this journey to think differently.

Part III
HOW

THINK DIFFERENTLY:

Their front feet have extra skin that acts like a paddle
when the animals are swimming. When platypuses are
on land, their webbing retracts, making the claws more
pronounced. The animals walk awkwardly on
their knuckles to protect this webbing.

(Bradford, 2014)

FIVE

GET CURIOUS

How to Notice Through Observation and Exploration

Explore the power to notice

Together, we are exploring our knowledge and skills to think differently. As we consider ourselves as learners and ask the question, "What do we value in learners?" we discover the "3i's" of engagement: independence, investment, and initiation.

Investment: The skills a learner demonstrates by showing that they are engaged and making meaningful connections to their experiences with the learning

Independence: The skills a learner demonstrates by doing something by themselves

Initiation: The skills a learner demonstrates by starting and persisting with learning

As we embark on our exploration to think differently, we will wonder together and ask ourselves to continuously reflect on our practices to enhance learner engagement. A question we will often ask ourselves is: How do we know a person is learning?

Let's dive into this question by asking more specifically about these "3i's" of engagement.

Is this individual **invested**, motivated, and has a purpose for engaging?

 Is this individual **independent**, has access to the experience, and shows fluency in routines?

Is the individual **initiating**, sharing knowledge, and seeking others for interaction?

Now that we have some questions to consider, we are going to want to also put on our "appreciation lenses." Yes, that's right; we are going to appreciate ourselves *and* our learners as we explore ways to replicate, reproduce, and expand things that are working across places and spaces of our practices.

Let's begin with this: How do you appreciate what's working? We tend to notice things when they are not working. Unfortunately, it's easier to see what's going wrong instead of what's going well, but with some intentionality, we can grow our livewired brains to think differently. Rather than saying, "I wish I had more time to review my notes before this meeting so I felt more prepared," you could say, "I notice when I read my notes before a meeting that I feel prepared." By using the phrase "I notice," you are seeing what's working and you are more likely to find the time to make it happen in the future, simply by acknowledging it in this way. How about this one: instead of saying, "I could use more lotion on my hands because they are so dry and cracked," you could say, "I notice when I use lotion on my hands because they stay soft." This tells me that lotion works, and I notice this because my hands are soft and free of cracks; therefore, lotion is what's working.

Here, give it a try. Refer to the examples shared above and write your own sentence. Use one of these phrases to get you started.

I wish …
I could…
I should …

Now, flip it. Write the comment through an appreciative inquiry lens of noticing. Use this phrase to start your statement.

I notice…

The way we say the words that we choose to use make an impact on how we notice. If you are interested in learning more about this idea, check out the work of Kegan and Lahey (2007), *How the Way We Talk Can Change the Way We Work: Seven Languages for Transformation*. I encourage you to check out other resources as you embark on this journey, as we may not take extensive time to review some concepts. Our focus is on noticing, on the appreciation of what we notice and how we notice it.

The knowledge of noticing and its impact

Now, take a look at your hand. What do you like about your hand? Did something that follows along the lines of, "I like the wrinkles on my hand, they show my age" or "I like my fingernails" come to mind? Or were thoughts like, "I like that my fingers don't have calluses on them" or "I like that my hands don't have too many wrinkles on them" the first to emerge? We tend to feel judgment when we like or dislike something. We tend to think that something is wrong or could be better. We tend to notice the flaws. Here's where the power of positive psychology comes into play. The way we appreciate begins with how we notice things, rather than how we like it.

Let's try this again. What do you notice about your hands? I notice that my hands are strong when I open the jar of pickles. I notice that my fingers move quickly when I type when I rest my palms to support my hands. I notice that my hands are soft when I use lotion to keep them moisturized.

Did you feel the difference? We can grow when we start with what we notice. Our negative thoughts and fear of judgment stay away, which allows us to move forward with a wondering, rather than a "shoulding." Shelley Moore (2018) argued that educators need to stop "shoulding" or comparing learners to an arbitrary norm. Instead, she suggested that we take learners where they are at and support them to determine their next steps.

Think about how it feels when someone gives you unsolicited input. It may feel like you are not enough, causing self-doubt. Maybe you start to question yourself and become paralyzed in your decision-making ability. That voice of shame echoes in your head saying, "It was okay, but it could be better if I try harder," when really there were parts that worked. When we choose to notice, rather than like or dislike, we can begin to wonder about how to grow into other places and spaces. Let's look at an example:

> *I notice that when I do a project for someone else, like making a photobook of our crazy hiking adventure together, I stick to a timeline and get it done so I can share it with them. I wonder if I'll stick to my own projects better if I invite someone to share with me?*

> *I notice my student is more engaged and organized in writing an opinion paper when they have a graphic organizer. I wonder if the quality of responses would increase in math if we used one [graphic organizer] to support explaining their answers?*

> *I notice that the learners are quiet during our transition from the science lecture to the lab when we incorporate music. When we stop the music to start the lecture, they are also quiet. I wonder if we can start class with increased learner engage-*

ment by playing music and then stop it when the bell rings?

Using an appreciative lens may feel a bit different than what you've done in the past, but it's an opportunity to think differently, to discover what's working, and to wonder where else it might work too.

Explore a different way with Appreciative Inquiry

The appreciative inquiry (AI) style, based on the research and concept initially introduced by David Cooperider in the business realm, encourages us to follow the "D's": define, discover, dream, design, and deliver/destiny. Cooperider (2012) shared that "desired change will never happen by solving yesterday's problems, but only by assembling 'a new combination of strengths' and then creating fresh designs that establish the new and eclipse the old." In learning, we are constantly discovering strengths, dreaming about innovative ideas, and designing something new based on what's working to deliver what's next.

Figure 5.1 The Appreciative Inquiry 4-D Approach

When using appreciative inquiry in education to support learners, we engage in a mentorship model with colleagues to explore the four "D's" to discover, dream, design and deliver. We have already defined our purpose—to enhance learner engagement; therefore, the "D" for define may be redundant and unnecessary in our work to think differently. Each of these is discrete for when we appreciate what is, to discover what works. When we dream to imagine what *could* be and design what *should* be, to connect and deliver what *will* be by taking action on what works. This can be done within a short amount of time because it connects to what is already in our practices. It is *not* something new. It **is** enhancing something we already do.

THINK DIFFERENTLY

VALUE YOURSELF

How to Use Appreciative Inquiry in a Peer-to-Peer Mentorship

Appreciate what is

Zooming out from the act of appreciative inquiry, we will also be exploring an approach known as the Social Emotional Engagement Knowledge and Skills (SEE-KS) framework. SEE-KS supports educators in implementing a relationship-oriented, curriculum-agnostic framework to ensure that learners are engaged in learning. This framework uses an appreciative inquiry approach with their mentorship six-step process to guide us in thinking differently. We will follow guidelines to navigate a proactive and emotionally regulating peer-to-peer mentorship session. This will allow us to have a collective discussion to appreciate "what's working" as we foster an ability to imagine "what could be" with the creation of an action plan (Rubin et al., 2015). The SEE-KS framework begins with the positive core of identifying a particular area that works with the belief that good is happening. It then enters the discovery phase to name it. Begin with finding a partner or a small group; this could be your professional learning community, the department team, or a grade-level team. Use Figure 6.1 guiding prompts to support the conversation as we begin to put it all together starting with the first "D": Discovery.

Figure 6.1 The Discovery Steps of the SEE-KS Framework

⌐DISCOVER
"NOTICE THE BEST OF WHAT IS."

1. **Identify your role and review the process of appreciative inquiry.**

   ❏ Share the purpose of this mentorship opportunity & our focus on appreciating the best of what is.

   ❏ Share that we will notice the "3i's" of engagement: *investment*, *independence*, and *initiation*.

2. **Invite the mentee(s) to start the inquiry conversation.**

   ❏ Begin by having the mentee describe the activity; what we are going to observe.

   ❏ Prompts to enhance the mentee to notice the best of <u>what is</u> might be:

      ○ Can you share the learning targets or goals?

      ○ Did you notice strategies that have been effective for learners' engagement?

   ❏ Share what you hear. *"So I heard you say... ," "Your goals were... ," "You mentioned... was working."*

3. **Discuss "what's working."**

   ❏ Use the notes gathered on the SEE-KS Mentorship Form to share <u>what is</u> noticed.

   ❏ Consider phrases that build upon what is observed to ensure appreciation *not flattery.*

      • "I notice that when ... occurs the learners demonstrate (this "3i" of engagement)."

      • "I hear learners share ideas about personal connections to the content by saying..."

      • "I see the learners leaning into their projects and shifting their gaze across various materials."

   (Rubin & Townsend, 2020)

As you engage in the discovery step, it is important to first identify your role and review the process of appreciative inquiry. Then, let the mentee start the conversation. Remember: this is about appreciation, and in this first step, you are engaging in the art of discovery. Listen with curiosity. By doing this, you're setting the norms of the mentorship interaction and creating the space for appreciation. An educator who embraces this process shared, "Appreciative inquiry and the SEE-KS process guides me to be more intentional in my reflections and helps me build on the strengths of what is already going well in my classroom." Let's take a look at this scenario to further explore the "D" of discovery:

> As an educator of 20 years, when I first got the email that I had been selected to be a part of this mentorship, I heard in my mind, "You are a failure." I said to myself that I did not need another person or another thing to tell me that I needed to do something better. So, that afternoon on my drive home from work, I was thinking more about this email, about how it read, "You will engage in the discovery of what is working to enhance learner engagement." I realized that this time might be different—at least, I hoped it would be. It kinda hit me and I told myself, "this is not being done to me rather this is being done with me." I remember that last year was one of the hardest in my career, and I often wished I had more support from my colleagues.

> So, as I started in this six-step mentorship, I thought the discovery—Steps 1 and 2—were going to be horrible. Recording myself was really terrifying. The idea of recording myself to share with my colleagues was even more anxiety-provoking. Yet, when I saw the video, I was relieved. I was relieved because I noticed the kids do exactly what I hoped they would. When I rang the windchime for their attention, they turned and looked at me for my direction. When I asked if a partner pair wanted to share their experiences with the class, two of my most disengaged learners shouted out "Yes, pick us!" while jumping up and down with their hands waving in the air. Watching the video showed me how in tune they were with me and how much they wanted to share their learning with each other. Seeing all their bodies turn in my direction and looking at me is not always what I felt in the classroom. Their

enthusiasm was often perceived in the moment as disruptive. To see it on video felt so remarkable. To know that what I am doing is working. Even the learner that I thought was often not paying attention turned to see what I had to say. To share this discovery with my colleagues felt so good, it was a breath of fresh air.

- 20-year experienced educator

Take a moment to reflect about how this discovery felt for this educator. Or, maybe you tried this yourself, in which case you can jot down your thoughts about the experience.

"*How did it feel to engage in this discovery?*"

Imagine what might be

As we continue on this learning journey, we are going to explore the second "D" in appreciative inquiry: dream. We will dream by imagining what *could* be. It will be important that unconscious barriers do not enter this part of the conversation as these will paralyze us. For example, have you ever played Pictionary? Grace Hawthorne, a professor at Stanford University Institute of Design, conducted a study with colleagues in which they used picture drawings to explore what happens to creativity under negative pressures.

Participants in the study were placed into a functional magnetic resonance imaging machine with a nonmagnetic tablet and asked to draw a series of pictures based on action words (for example, vote, exhaust, salute) with 30 seconds for each word. (They also drew a zigzag line to establish baseline brain function for the task of drawing.) The participants later ranked each word picture based on its difficulty to draw. The tablet transmitted the drawings to researchers at the school who

THINK DIFFERENTLY

scored them on a 5-point scale of creativity, and researchers at the School of Medicine analyzed the fMRI scans for brain activity patterns.

The results were surprising: the prefrontal cortex, traditionally associated with thinking, was most active for the drawings the participants ranked as most difficult; the cerebellum [the part of the brain traditionally associated with movement] was most active for the drawings the participants scored highest on for creativity. Essentially, the less the participants thought about what they were drawing, the more creative their drawings were.

(Saggar et al., 2016, p. 3545)

These findings share that overthinking makes it harder to do your best creative work. Researcher Jessica Schmerler echoed this conclusion in her *Science America* article "Don't Overthink It, Less Is More When It Comes to Creativity" (Schemerler, 2015). Education is creative work, and so is dreaming. It takes work to stay in the dreamer mindset of what *might* be. Dreaming is a part of letting the unconscious mind go to work—to push aside the barriers that we know exist and allow your knowledge to flow in a creative way. This may feel a bit silly or maybe unproductive at first, but stick with it. In Steps 3 and 4, you will use your skills to notice and wonder. The prompts in Figure 6.2 will guide you in the discussion. It is important to use comments of appreciation and not flattery. Follow the prompts given to discuss what is working and inquiry about which of the "3i's" we want to explore further.

Figure 6.2 The Dream Step of the SEE-KS Framework

△DREAM

"IMAGINE WHAT MIGHT BE."

4. **Inquire about which of the "3i's" of engagement the mentee[s] would like to explore.**

❏ Imagine <u>what might be</u> by encouraging the mentee to consider ways to enhance what's working and brainstorm as if anything is possible.

❏ If there is uncertainty, consider asking what do you *hope for... dream for* with your learners?"

(Rubin & Townsend, 2020)

The ideas generated in these steps become the catapult for enhancing what works. Let's take a look at this scenario to further explore the "D" of dreaming.

> *As an educator, I feel that learners today are all about technology, and I notice that when I incorporate opportunities to use tech and work with their peers, learners are more engaged. I also notice that when I model the strategy for the learners and use chart paper, the product I make becomes permanent. The chart paper is a tool that learners can refer back to during their partner or independent work times. They can come back to it. I notice that the learners in my class seem to like to sit on the carpet and come upfront for our group learning opportunities.*

> *I feel like engaging the learners that seem disengaged, looking off how to connect with learners on the perimeter—like their body is in the group, but their brain seems to be somewhere else. As I watched the video and shifted my perspective to appreciate what works, I began to notice opportunities where I could hook them in this learning. I want to focus on, "How do I use 'just-right' peer opportunities to connect with learner interests and enhance their investment in our partner work?"*

In a dreamer's world where no barriers exist, I imagine each kid having their device where I can airdrop images of our anchor charts to them, so when they do partner work, they can mark it up. Or when we come back together as a group, I have a smart TV for them to airplay onto and share their work with peers. I know that some learners are quiet, more introverted— and that is okay, because in a dreamer's world, I can use QR codes for learners to scan. These codes can help them ask their peers a question or prompt them to a visual that has sentence starters for their peer conversations.

There are moments in other parts of our day that I sing a line in a song—specifically, Aretha's RESPECT—and they are all so invested in this moment. I'm not sure if it's my great singing or because I'm not the best singer, but they are paying attention. Maybe because we do our think-pair-share so often, I could add a song to this time in our day too. Wow, this was amazing to dream about, and I actually think there are things I've shared that I can put into action.

- 3-year experienced educator

How did dreaming feel? Consider the scenario or maybe in your own dreaming conversations. Did it feel unrealistic, hard, overwhelming, exciting, fun, or invigorating to think about all that could be? How did it feel to dream about the strategies that are effective and to generate ideas to creatively enhance what works? Take a moment to reflect about how this dreaming felt for this educator or your thoughts about the experience.

"*How did it feel to dream?*"

Determine what could be

We are entering the third "D" in appreciative inquiry: design. This is where we review our discoveries from Step 1 and narrow down the ideas that we just generated in the dreaming phase. Next, through the review of our discovery, we narrow down the ideas generated in the dreaming phase. Remember that you have experience and knowledge that will guide you in designing a realistic next step. Think about what you can reasonably do within the next 4 days. It is important to plan out the action that you will take next in this design phase. You can use the following prompts to help you think differently:

- "I noticed how effective it was when....
- "How might this look during [this part]?"
- "I wonder if...."

Keep in mind, you don't need to design the "right answer" or have an "expert" tell you what you should be doing. This part of the process inherently provides an opportunity to design what "should be" based on what you know to be working and the possibilities of what "can be." This is opposed to the more traditional and coercive mechanisms for planned change. You can refer to Figure 6.3 to help guide your design thinking.

Figure 6.3 The Design Step of the SEE-KS Framework

⚠DESIGN

"DETERMINE WHAT COULD BE."

5. **Collaborate to discuss what possible "actions" may be to enhance what's working.**

❑ Reflect back on the notes taken in the discovery of what's working and think about <u>what could be</u>.

❑ Consider ways to connect the discovery of what's working with the inquiry of what might be to design learning experiences that enhance engagement, remember your hopes and dreams for learners.

❑ Comments might include, "I noticed when.... how might this look if...?" or "I wonder if...."

(Rubin & Townsend, 2020)

Based on the educator's input during the dreaming phase of appreciative inquiry, let's take a look at the continuation of the scenario:

Given the ideas generated during the dreaming of what could be, I am ready to design what should be. In the design I think adding music into our learning and having learners be a part of the lyrics will be a great way to keep them invested. We can connect the lyric writing to our poetry unit and then put it to a familiar song. I also feel that my team and I can collaborate to design some resources for kids that will help them initiate more with their peer partners. We can create QR codes and put these around the room or on a bookmark tool for them to easily access. I do feel that although we may not always have a device that can airplay, we do use Google Suite and I can ask a learner to take a photo of our chart paper and upload it to our electronically shared classroom folders. Then, if learners want to use it while working with their peer partners, they have it as an option. I think this could be what we do next based on what is working, and it will help me to use 'just-right' peer opportunities to connect learner interests and ultimately enhance their investment in learning. The lyrics in the song will support their understanding of what working with a peer looks like and sounds like. The QR codes will give them access to tools that they can use during their partner work. When I do this, their engagement will increase. There are so many opportunities to engage in partner work that I think the time investment on my end is worth it. I look forward to the next step in this inquiry process.

"How did it feel to design what should be using appreciative inquiry?"

I'm wondering how the design step felt, either just to yourself while you were reading or in your conversations with others. Did determining what "should be" feel inviting, engaging, satisfying or productive? How did it feel to enhance your design of strategies? What about designing ideas that complement what already works? I invite you to take a moment to reflect on how determining what "should be" felt compares to your prior experiences.

Deliver what will be

The fourth "D" in appreciative inquiry asks us to create what will be. This is our last step: delivery. Remember that in our design phase, we framed our thinking around what could be done within the next 4 days. We will need to be honest with ourselves. Here, you have the opportunity to set up some accountability for yourself and to invite your colleague or trusted partner to support you by assigning responsibilities. Now is your time to design what "will be." We know that having a plan and using our executive functioning skills to break the plan into manageable steps is critical to success. Figure 6.4 gives a framework for the delivery phase and invites us to create the accountability needed to deliver. Use a strategy here that works for you. Think about what tools and resources

THINK DIFFERENTLY

you have used in the past to take action and use them. This is your time to shine, to organize the steps needed in this enhanced design of what "will be" so that you can deliver it.

Figure 6.4 The Deliver Step of the SEE-KS Framework

⏷DELIVER
"TAKE ACTION ON WHAT WILL BE."

6. **Identify a plan and select the "next steps."**

❏ It's time to create <u>what will be</u> put into action. What will be created, used in the learning to enhance the "3i's" of engagement and identify the supports you desire to make it a reality.

❏ Consider "Do you have an opportunity where you think you might try this in the near future?"

(Rubin & Townsend, 2020)

In this scenario, the educator identified that she works well when using "I will" statements and having someone to share her product with. Let's take a look at how she develops an action plan of next steps.

In the design phase, it was determined that I will develop and enhance the following:

Use music to support partner work expectations—I will support the learners to develop lyrics for a partner work song. The lyrics will explain what partner work looks like and sounds like. I will do this with the class in writing on Thursday.

❏ *Create a graphic organizer for learners to use when generating ideas.*

❏ *What does partner work look like? List attributes you will see in yourself or your partner while collaborating.*

❏ *What does partner work sound like? List words or phrases you might hear while doing partner work that support the learning.*

❏ *Create a playlist of songs that we can choose from to apply the lyrics.*

Enhance learning tools to support initiation between peers during partner work.

❏ *Connect with my colleagues, specifically the speech pathologist to collaboratively develop learning tools.*

    ❏ *Create a video model of partner work.*

    ❏ *Create the bookmarks that will give learners sentence starters.*

❏ *Create an opportunity for a learner in the class to be the photographer of our charts and upload them to our electronically shared folder.*

❏ *Use a QR code generator to link the tools developed and share them with the learners to access when doing partner work.*

I know that some of these resources already exist, and by collaborating with my colleagues, we can adjust some of the tools we are already using. I also recognize that when I involve learners in the creative process of these resources, they become more invested. I know this connects with our literacy unit and fits into the lesson plan later in the week.

I'm wondering how the delivery phase felt—either just to yourself while reading or in your discussions with others. Did determining what "will be" feel peaceful, doable, manageable, exciting, nice, or reassuring? How did it feel to make the plan for your enhanced design, tying together strategies that are effective and complement what already works? Take a moment to reflect about how you are delivering what "will be" in comparison to prior experiences.

Listen to part of someone's story

"How did it feel to make the plan for what "will be" designed?"

Using an appreciative inquiry-based model such as the one shared in SEE-KS to look at our educational practices gives us a professional learning approach that respects the educators' knowledge and skills and supports how we engage with one another to enhance all learners' social emotional engagement in learning. The appendices provide examples of how this all comes together using the six-step mentorship and the mentorship form.

Here's what educators have stated on this practice:

> "I really feel validated as an educator. I feel like my teaching has grown so much just because I'm working on something that I want to work on. I'm excited to teach."
>
> - 20-year experienced elementary school educator

> "I was suspicious at first wondering why we were changing a practice [coaching]. We had already been doing it, but the fact is, after going through the process I feel so validated. I feel a part of the process. I feel in control, and I feel appreciated."
>
> - 5-year experienced elementary school educator

> "I feel this melded everything else that we are doing together, and it supports us to take a step back and appreciate what's going well—which, as an educator, we just don't do enough of."
>
> - 12-year experienced middle school educator

This quote is from an educator who explored using the four "D's" with the learners in her class:

> "With our classroom vision *to build access in different ways to*

increase a sense of belonging and inclusiveness to our class-room community, I asked the students to list out things they have seen work towards this vision. Then, we dreamed together. One student talked about the stations we used, another student added to this and then another and another. They were fully into this dream with me. What was super cool is that students talked about the access THEY needed for themselves as often as they talked about access that might be needed for others and how they too benefited from these options. Applying the four "D's" to my practice was game-changing but hearing how students shared when I applied it to their learning creates a real potential to exponentially change the work we can do together."

- 15-year experienced high school educator

These stories encourage us to stay curious, to notice what's working, and to apply appreciative inquiry to enhance learner engagement and our own self-efficacy.

Find connections with positivity

Sometimes, we may find ourselves reaching out for the support we need. Other times, we find ourselves as the recipients of unsolicited coaching, and this can feel a lot like being told what to do. We may be on the receiving end of phrases like "Here, I'll do it. Let me show you." While there may be a time and place, this kind of interaction can leave you feeling like the learning is being done to you, especially when you didn't initiate the interaction in the first place. When we're teaching, we too can get caught up in what curriculum is taught, the pressures to follow our scope and sequence, and what we must impart onto our learners that we forget these are useless without connection. As Master Yoda (2020) says, "In connection, strength we find, and happen, great things can." When we value ourselves and invite conversation through our connections with others, it becomes an opportunity to flourish. We can hone our knowledge, skills, and disposition in order to grow, nurture relationships, and connect to one another in a positive, meaningful, and purposeful way. In doing this, we will enhance what we are doing that works for our learners and feel inspired to continue moving forward. That said, I invite you to think about who you have connections with and ask yourself, "Do they support me in finding the strengths in myself and my practices?"

PAUSE HERE AND COMPLETE THIS DISCOVERY SENTENCE:

I am curious about…

And I want to notice what's working so I can grow in this area.

NOW, LET'S DREAM BY COMPLETING THIS SENTENCE:

If no barriers existed and all resources were available, this might look like…

Now, imagine what happens when we use an appreciative inquiry-based approach to notice our skills and make a choice to engage with the four "D's": discover, dream, design, and deliver an action that will boost our engagement.

Flip the flattery of judgment

We get noticed many times by others. Of those times, I wonder how many feel good, how many feel bad, and why? There is this unconscious thing that happens when we hear someone notice us and why it might feel good or bad: judgment. When we are seen by others, it sometimes feels like they are noticing us just to judge us, whereas other times it feels appreciative. Why? It's all about the approach. When someone starts a phrase with "I like…" or "Where did you get…?" or "What a nice…," it tends to feel more judgmental. In contrast, when someone starts a phrase with "I notice...," "I see...," or "I heard...," we hear an invitation. We have to hone our skills of noticing through observation in order to appreciate—rather than give flattery or judgment.

Make it observable

There are many ways to approach the action of observing. I find that with clarification of what we are looking for, we will have more success at seeing it. With that in mind, let's explore something that we may all be familiar with: writing goals. Have you ever written a goal that when you look back at it, you are really not sure what you were hoping to achieve when this goal is met? Maybe it was too broad, lofty, unclear, or lacked measurable aspects. I wonder, have you written a goal for a learner that says to stay on task? The idea of staying on task can be extremely broad, and what you might see could look vastly different based on many variables and perceptions. Our prior experiences, biases, and cultures support us to process what we have learned. Many of us believe that we are staying on task, and when someone else says we are "off task," it seems a bit odd. In reality, the opportunity is that we need to think about what we see that tells us we are paying attention or what we hear that tells us someone is on task. What does that look like?

Take a moment here to think about a reality television game called *Minute to Win It* (Banner et al., 2010). In this game there are specific instructions, time limits, and materials presented with specific parameters that will determine whether the participants successfully demonstrate the skill. For example:

> "In this challenge, contestants will be doubles partners and participate in a game of office tennis using clipboards as rackets. The couple must crumple a paper ball and pass it back and forth to get it into the wastebasket on the opposite side of the stage. If either player double hits or carries the paper ball, the line judge will nullify the point. Failure to do this task within 60 seconds or less may result in elimination."

THINK DIFFERENTLY

Office Tennis Minute to Win It Challenge (Banner et al., 2010).

When we break apart this challenge, it can be put into a goal template. Let's try this format of thinking when generating a goal. *Given* items, *the person will* demonstrate an action, *by* doing something, *with* these parameters of time for a certain number of opportunities and possibly in different environments or with various people. For example:

> *Given* a clipboard as a racket, a crumpled paper ball and a wastebasket, *the partners will* pass the paper ball back and forth to move it across the stage (without double hits or carries) *by* <u>using the clipboard to tap the paper ball in a turn-taking (back and forth) format</u> *across* 15 feet, <u>five times within 60 seconds or less.</u>

The underlined information is what we can see, observe, and measure in this goal to gather the data. The italic information can be keywords to support the structure of the goal. The other information is valuable for clarity in observing and noticing the desired actions and supports that will enhance the successful outcomes when this goal is met.

Data Collection System										
Use the clipboard to T-tap, C-carry, D-double hit										
Paper ball successfully in wastebasket ✔yes, X no)										
Time to complete the task: ❏ <60 seconds ❏> 60 seconds										
Turn Taking ❏ Yes ❏ No										

Sometimes we collect too much data, while other times we write a goal in which is hard to figure out what skill we are working on or how to measure it. This different way of thinking about goals provides us with the structure and may support how we measure and keep ourselves accountable. Give it a try. Google a *Minute to Win It* game or think about a goal you have for yourself or someone else you are supporting.

NOW, IT'S YOUR TURN TO GIVE THIS STYLE OF GOAL WRITING A TRY.

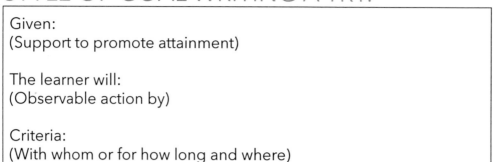

Given:
(Support to promote attainment)

The learner will:
(Observable action by)

Criteria:
(With whom or for how long and where)

The next step is to <u>underline</u> the measurable components in the goal. This will become the data that you will collect to measure progress.

FINALLY, BASED ON THE UNDERLINED INFORMATION IN THE GOAL, CREATE A DATA COLLECTION SYSTEM.

Here are a few examples of some goal writing and data collection. These goals are written based on the present level of performance, which drives this opportunity. There are many ways to write goals and various ideas for how to measure them; this is just one way to do it. It is important to follow local guidelines when writing goals in legal documents.

EXAMPLE A.

Given: a visual cue and a visual dictionary of gestures along with close proximity to peers.

The learner will: <u>initiate</u> with and <u>respond</u> to peers during <u>familiar routines</u>

Criteria: with three peers across four school <u>environments</u> on 4 out of 5 opportunities.

Data Collection
  Close proximity to peers: ❏ Yes, ❏ No
  Routine: ❏ Familiar, ❏ Unfamiliar
  Learner Action: ❏ Initiate, ❏ Respond
  Peer: _____   Environment: _____
  Additional Notes (comments, topics, other noticings, etc.):

EXAMPLE B.

Given: access to visual learning strategies in self-awareness and self-management paired with on-going opportunities with peers

The learner will: recognize a desire to <u>share</u> with others by raising her hand, walking towards a peer, or securing the other person's attention and making a comment to share possibly using <u>use a strategy</u>

Criteria: on 4 out of 5 measured opportunities across 9 consecutive classes.

Data:
  Seeks out someone to share with by *initiating*
          Numerical Scale: fully supported
          1 – 2 – 3 – 4 – 5 fully independent
  Action observed: ❏ Raise hand ❏ Walk towards
  ❏ Secures attention ❏ Comments
  Strategy used: ❏ Graphic organizer ❏ Visual timer
  ❏ Screen reader ❏ other __ ❏ n/a

Now, you have the concept of how to make it observable and are exploring the need to develop a data collection system to confirm that it can be measured. Let's go back to the idea that sometimes we ask or desire for others to pay attention or stay on task. Thinking about this goal writing exercise we did; you might have a visual of what that looks like to you. I wonder if others think it will look the same. Even more importantly, I'm curious if the person performing the task or asked to pay attention has been asked "What does it look like for you to pay attention?" or "Do they know what it looks like or sounds like in a particular scenario?" You may need to dig deeper and ask yourself, "What will I see, what will I hear?" if you desire someone to pay attention and listen. If you thought, "I notice someone is paying attention when their eye gaze is towards the speaker and they're responding with gestures or actions that match the context," that makes an image we can see and hear in our minds.

Creating this type of definition is sometimes referred to as an operational definition. An operational definition, as it relates to an action or behavior, is a description of what something looks like in a way that is observable, measurable, and repeatable (Metcalf et al., 2017). When this type of definition is used, it also creates curiosity because if the person's gaze is away from the speaker you can discover ideas to support them. Eye gaze is observable, it is measurable, and it can be repeated as well as shaped over time by using the information gathered. Let's take another example here: consider if the person is not yet responding with gestures or actions you can provide opportunities to observe others' gestures or actions when there is a definition of what we are looking for or what we hope to see. This becomes the opportunity to teach some of these gestures in a direct manner. If I stopped at the initial statement of "pay attention" instead, I may not have been curious enough to discover the observable actions of what I might see, hear, or notice that tells others someone is focused and also have the respect of how the act of paying attention may look different for each of us, but it can be defined for each of us so that it is observable, measurable, and repeatable.

Let's practice. Review these following statements and think about what you notice. Could someone else notice it in a similar way, or is it too broad and may need to be more specific?

UNDERLINE OR HIGHLIGHT WHAT YOU CAN NOTICE (OBSERVE):

I see a neighbor walking down the sidewalk.
I notice two friends sharing a secret.
I see the kid is paying attention.
I hear a child singing in the stairwell.
I notice that boy is off task and not doing his work.

If you underlined the verbs "walking," "sharing," or "singing," that is a good start; however, "paying attention" or "doing work" are also actions that are just harder to see in the same way. Yes, we can see "walking," we can hear "singing," but *what* will we see that tells us "sharing"? It's important that we define what actions such as these look like and sound like if we are going to measure them by recording data on them to determine a level of performance for another individual.

"Where have I seen a goal that I may consider more clearly defining?"

What does "paying attention" look like and sound like? What does being "on task" look like and sound like, and does the person being asked to demonstrate these skills have an understanding of them? A goal is a plan for how one will demonstrate and measure a skill. By writing them, our task becomes to notice them. Specifically, we must notice what's working, appreciate it, and enhance opportunities to generalize the skill so that learners can demonstrate their "3i's" of engagement through showing investment, independence, and initiation.

Side note: when we focus on negative actions, we notice them more. Continuing to think differently will be hard at times, as this may challenge the status quo and go against some deeply-rooted biases and educational climates, but I promise that we will notice the actions we desire to see if we focus on them more. There is time and space for observing undesirable actions, but that is not our focus right now. If you are interested in thinking differently about less desirable actions, or what we most commonly call "behaviors," I would encourage you to read the work of Julie Causton and Kate Macleod's (2020) *From Behavior to Belonging*. It will completely blow your mind and warm your heart.

Recap and ideas to consider

Our next step is to try some of these ways of thinking by writing a goal in a different way, gathering usable data, capturing ourselves in action, and asking others to join-in to appreciate you and return the gesture. This is the part where the true opportunity is in your hands to appreciate and inquire to determine what happens next. Educators will grow and nurture practices in a manner that will strengthen what is already working through the use of an appreciative model. Social Emotional Engagement – Knowledge and Skills (SEE-KS) is one way in which focuses on providing a mechanism to enhance the provision of educational programming for all learners. This is done by creating a universal design for learning, with an emphasis on the social emotional well-being and self-efficacy of both the educators and the learners alike.

"Where will I make the commitment for myself to think differently?"

By using the principles of appreciative inquiry to discover, dream, design, and deliver, we can guide a collective discussion about what's working and create an action plan for next steps that you, as the educator, truly want to do because you feel passionate about it and are invested in emphasizing what's already working. Who wouldn't want to do more of a good thing? Additionally, the professional learning structures here are designed to engage a transdisciplinary audience as a means to build capacity within each system for professional learning, training, coaching, and peer-to-peer mentorship. This will not be an expert coming in to tell you what to do. Rather, someone will be in the trenches with, supporting you; in return, you get to support them because this is a peer-to-peer mentorship. If you choose to seek out the expert, there's an opportunity here too in sharing the four "D's" of appreciative inquiry to have a collaborative conversation. There is time and place for an expert-based model; however, in our work, here this is not the driving force. Use the appendices to find and play with the resources that we explored in our learning to use an appreciative inquiry process in your educational practices. Oh, and skim through the references too, as they are what got me to this point in sharing this information with you.

The appreciative inquiry approach supports us to stay curious as we continue to invite others to join us in noticing and wondering, to empathize, not solve, and remain compassionate for ourselves and others. A well-informed yoga leader once shared, "When we truly get to know ourselves and respect ourselves, I truly believe the world is a better place" (Yoga with Adriene, 2019). Together, we can share appreciation and truly respect ourselves in the process. Lastly, I'll leave you with this quote from American philosopher and psychologist William James: "The deepest principle in human nature is the craving to be appreciated." Thank you for going on this learning journey with me. It is my sincerest hope that you embrace the ideas shared and choose to think differently. I wholeheartedly believe that together, we will do more than *make* a difference; through appreciation of one another and ourselves, we will *be* the difference.

THINK DIFFERENTLY

Appendices

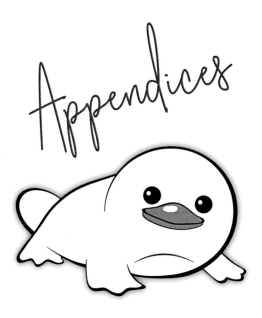

THINK DIFFERENTLY:

The platypus is described as one of the most unusual creatures in the animal kingdom. Platypuses (which is the correct plural form, not "platypi") have a paddle-shaped tail like a beaver; a sleek, furry body like an otter; and a flat bill and webbed feet like a duck.

(Bradford, 2014)

Appendix A: Appreciative Inquiry Mentorship Bookmark

Social Emotional Engagement Knowledge and Skills (SEE-KS)
www.see-ks.com

Appreciative Inquiry Mentorship

Comments to Support **4D**ISCOVERY

"I notice when ... occurs, the learners demonstrate this... "3i's" of engagement."

"I hear learners share ideas about personal connections to the content by saying... and this seems to show "3i's of engagement.""

"I see learners physically leaning into their projects and shifting their gaze at various materials, to show "3i's" of engagement."

Comments to Support **4D**ESIGN

"Considering what's working, could we enhance a "3i's" of engagement if..."

"I'm wondering, based on what we noticed and what we dreamed might be, could we consider this "3i's" of engagement by..."

The Mentorship Guidelines

① **Identify** mentorship roles and review the process of <u>appreciative inquiry</u> to notice the "3i's" of engagement and the best of what is.

4DISCOVERY ② **Invite** the mentee to start the conversation by describing the activity, sharing the learning targets or goals and notice moments where strategies have been effective for engagement. ③ **Discuss** the best of <u>what is</u> by using the SEE-KS Mentorship Form as a guide. *Flip this bookmark over for comments to support.*

4DREAM ④ **Inquire** about which of the "3i's" of engagement to explore through imagining <u>what might be</u> by considering ways to enhance what works and brainstorm as if anything is possible.

4DESIGN ⑤ **Collaborate** to discuss <u>what could be</u> and the possible "actions" that may be taken to enhance what's working.

4DELIVER ⑥ **Create** a plan and select the next steps to develop <u>what will be</u> and identify the supports you desire to make it a reality.

SEE-KS Mentorship Steps ① ② ③ ④ ⑤ ⑥

THINK DIFFERENTLY

Appendix B: CASEL Social and Emotional Learning (SEL) Competencies

SOCIAL AND EMOTIONAL LEARNING (SEL) COMPETENCIES

SELF-AWARENESS

The ability to accurately recognize one's own emotions, thoughts, and values and how they influence behavior. The ability to accurately assess one's strengths and limitations, with a well-grounded sense of confidence, optimism, and a "growth mindset."

- ⇒ IDENTIFYING EMOTIONS
- ⇒ ACCURATE SELF-PERCEPTION
- ⇒ RECOGNIZING STRENGTHS
- ⇒ SELF-CONFIDENCE
- ⇒ SELF-EFFICACY

SOCIAL AWARENESS

The ability to take the perspective of and empathize with others, including those from diverse backgrounds and cultures. The ability to understand social and ethical norms for behavior and to recognize family, school, and community resources and supports.

- ⇒ PERSPECTIVE-TAKING
- ⇒ EMPATHY
- ⇒ APPRECIATING DIVERSITY
- ⇒ RESPECT FOR OTHERS

RESPONSIBLE DECISION-MAKING

The ability to make constructive choices about personal behavior and social interactions based on ethical standards, safety concerns, and social norms. The realistic evaluation of consequences of various actions, and a consideration of the well-being of oneself and others.

- ⇒ IDENTIFYING PROBLEMS
- ⇒ ANALYZING SITUATIONS
- ⇒ SOLVING PROBLEMS
- ⇒ EVALUATING
- ⇒ REFLECTING
- ⇒ ETHICAL RESPONSIBILITY

SELF-MANAGEMENT

The ability to successfully regulate one's emotions, thoughts, and behaviors in different situations — effectively managing stress, controlling impulses, and motivating oneself. The ability to set and work toward personal and academic goals.

- ⇒ IMPULSE CONTROL
- ⇒ STRESS MANAGEMENT
- ⇒ SELF-DISCIPLINE
- ⇒ SELF-MOTIVATION
- ⇒ GOAL SETTING
- ⇒ ORGANIZATIONAL SKILLS

RELATIONSHIP SKILLS

The ability to establish and maintain heal and rewarding relationships with diverse viduals and groups. The ability to commu clearly, listen well, cooperate with others inappropriate social pressure, negotiate constructively, and seek and offer help w needed.

- ⇒ COMMUNICATION
- ⇒ SOCIAL ENGAGEMENT
- ⇒ RELATIONSHIP BUILDING
- ⇒ TEAMWORK

Social and Emotional Learning (SEL) Competencies: ©2021 CASEL. All Rights Reserved. [https://www.casel.org/wp-content/uploads/2017/08/Sample-Teaching-Activities-to-Support-Core-Competencies-8-20-17.pdf]

Appendix C: CAST Universal Design for Learning Guidelines 2.2

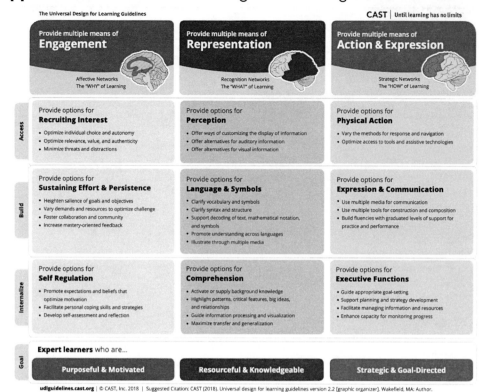

CAST. (2018). *Universal design for learning guidelines version 2.2 [graphic organizer]*. Author.

Appendix D: Plan for Implementation and Sustainability (SEE-KS)

SEE-KS in Action
A Plan for Implementation and Sustainability

☐ Before the school year starts

Define what you want to do this upcoming year.
Consider asking your team some questions.
   "What worked in the past?" "What do we want to continue?"
   "Where do we want to grow?" "How will we know if we are successful?"

Develop statements that will support this work.
Consider using an "if, then" format. "If we do this... then we will see that..."

```

```

Collaborative Mentorships: If we utilize and build upon the expertise of our staff by involving all team members (teacher, special education teacher, aides, student services) by scheduling and committing to regular collaborative mentorship conversations surrounding the social, emotional, and academic needs of our learners, then we will be able to enhance the "3i's" of engagement by aligning, designing and delivering a universally designed inclusive education experience that support the social emotional engagement of all learners and educators. We will know this to be true by using SEE-KS pre and post reflection and measurement tools, our building site data for student attendance, office referrals, the overall teacher retention rates and our community's input.

Draft the vision.
Dream big and use brainstorming techniques to bring a vision to light. Think about your purpose and the goals you plan to achieve. Then sprinkle in some values and that's your vision. Now put it all together and make it flow. You may end up with a longer vision and if that's the case you'll want to have a brief vision statement for your team to recall more easily. The more people know the vision the more inline we will be as a team working towards a shared vision.

```

```

Vision of The Best School:
To be a place that appreciates the design, creation and engagement in learning together.

SEE-KS

SEE-KS in Action
A Plan for Implementation and Sustainability

Extended Vision of the Best School
At The Best School, learners, educators, staff and families feel valued and heard. We empower one another to explore learning in creative, fun, and engaging ways to reach our full potential by enhancing the "3i's" of engagement. We believe in creating an environment where everyone belongs, feels safe and accepted for our differences. We do all of this with respect for ourselves and one another. We value a community of collaboration and appreciation for all perspectives.

Map out the plan for action
Discover possible entry points by considering current structures within the system such as professional learning communities, department meetings, grade level collaboration, professional learning days, etc.

The plan of action for the Best School:
Using our PLC structure - At one of the weekly professional learning community (PLC) collaborative meetings per month we will use the SEE-KS Mentorship Guidelines to engage in appreciative discussions to grow our knowledge and skills in how we universally designed learning experiences that enhance the "3i's" of engagement.

Using our Professional Learning Days - Educators will be given options to engage in learning about the social neuroscience of engagement for learning. Collectively we will learn about SEE-KS: Why, What and How through a traditional presentation model and will be given options to participate on-going learning including a book study, attend webinars, virtual mentorships, or other related experiences that may be presented by an educator that we have not thought of yet.

SEE-KS

SEE-KS in Action

A Plan for Implementation and Sustainability

☐ During the school year

Quarter 1

❏ Attend SEE-KS: Why, What & How professional learning.
> A professional learning experience that explores the social neuroscience of engagement, discovers measures for learner engagement and shares how we support educators to enhance what works positively impacts our social, emotional and academic outcomes.

❏ Host a "lunch and learn" with the SEE-KS tools and resources.

❏ Collect data related to statement(s) to support this work that may include educator pre self-reflection, learner engagement and the sustainability measurement tools, our building site data for attendance, office referrals and other related data per our statements.

❏ Propose book study books and develop book groups.

❏ Select dates for appreciative discussions using the SEE-KS Mentorship Guidelines.

PLC Dates & Educator Mentorships *(Educator will be named for this example A-F)*			
October 13th	November 10th	December 8th	January 12th
Mentorship Focus: Educator A & B	Delivery Update: Educator A & B	Delivery Update: Educator C & D	Delivery Update: Educator E, F
Collaborators: Educator C, D, E, F	Mentorship Focus: Educator C & D	Mentorship Focus: Educator E & F	PLC reflection in these mentorships
	Collaborators: Educator E, F, A, B	Collaborators: Educator A, B, C, D	Review SEE-KS tools and data opportunities
February 9th	March 9th	April 13th	May 11th
Mentorship Focus: Educator B & A	Delivery Update: Educator B & A	Delivery Update: Educator D & C	Delivery Updates: Educator F & E
Collaborators: Educator C, D, E, F	Mentorship Focus: Educator D & C	Mentorship Focus: Educator F & E	Review SEE-KS tools and update data
	Collaborators: Educator E, F, A, B	Collaborators: Educator A, B, C, D	Celebrations and Reflections

SEE-KS

SEE-KS in Action

A Plan for Implementation and Sustainability

☐ Reflecting on the school year

Review what you did this year. Consider asking your team some questions.
"What worked for us?"
"What do we want to continue?"
"How do we know we were successful?"
"Where do we want to go next?"

```



```

Reflections from The Best School:

"What worked for us?" Having the time built into our already existing structure of the PLC worked well as we were able to focus once a month on this style of collaboration.
"What do we want to continue?" Being able to learn about the social neuroscience in learning through the SEE-KS why, what and how professional development has made us curious and we want to continue to grow our learning.

"How do we know we were successful?" Our data shows this success. We've seen an overall decline in office referrals and increase in our student attendance as well as our staff attendance. We have a pulse in our building that truly exudes our vision and our data supports this feeling.

"Where do we want to go next?" We want to continue using the SEE-KS Mentorship Guidelines as a PLC. We also want to support our learners to know more about themselves. To have an understanding of the neuroscience in learning, to be designers alongside us [educators] and to notice in themselves the "3i's" of engagement.

We also want to note that connections to statewide, district and school initiatives were made whenever feasible so that this work did not feel like one-more-thing rather it was a part of what we already do.

SEE-KS

THINK DIFFERENTLY

Appendix E: SEE-KS Mentorship Guidelines: The 6-Step Process of Appreciative Inquiry

SEE-KS ⬡
The Mentorship Guidelines
The 6-Step Process of Appreciative Inquiry

ISCOVER
REAM
ESIGN
ELIVER

SEE-KS uses the philosophy of appreciative inquiry to guide our mentorship. A collective discussion of "what's working" fosters an ability to imagine "what might be" and the creation of the actions for "what will be." The following guidelines foster a positive, productive and emotionally regulating peer-to-peer mentorship session.

Mark-off the 6-Steps as you move through the SEE-KS appreciative inquiry process: ① ② ③ ④ ⑤ ⑥

---

① **Identify your role and review the process of appreciative inquiry.**
- ❏ Share the purpose of this mentorship opportunity and our focus on appreciating the best of what is.
- ❏ Share that we will notice the "3i's" of engagement: *investment, independence,* and *initiation.*

D ISCOVERY
② **Invite the mentee(s) to start the inquiry conversation.**
- ❏ Begin by having the mentee describe the activity; what we are going to observe.
- ❏ Prompts to enhance the mentee to notice the best of <u>what is</u> might be:
    - o Can you share the learning targets or goals?
    - o Did you notice strategies that have been effective for learners' engagement?
- ❏ Share what you hear. *"So I heard you say…," "Your goals were…," "You mentioned… was working."*

③ **Discuss "what's working."**
- ❏ Use the notes gathered on the SEE-KS Mentorship Form to share <u>what is</u> noticed.
- ❏ Consider phrases that build upon what is observed to ensure appreciation *not flattery.*
    - • "I notice when … occurs the learners demonstrate (this "3i" of engagement)."
    - • "I hear learners share ideas about personal connections to the content by saying…"
    - • "I see the learners leaning into their projects and shifting their gaze across various materials."

D REAM
④ **Inquire about which of the "3i's" of engagement the mentee[s] would like to explore.**
- ❏ Imagine <u>what might be</u> by encouraging the mentee to consider ways to enhance what's working and brainstorm as if anything is possible.
- ❏ If there is uncertainty, consider asking what do you *hope for… dream for* with your learners?"

D ESIGN
⑤ **Collaborate to discuss what possible "actions" may be to enhance what's working.**
- ❏ Reflect back on the notes taken in the discovery of what's working and think about <u>what could be.</u>
- ❏ Consider ways to connect the discovery of what's working with the inquiry of what might be to design learning experiences that enhance engagement, remember your hopes and dreams for learners.
- ❏ Comments might include, "I noticed when…. how might this look if…?" or "I wonder if…."

D ELIVER
⑥ **Identify a plan and select the "next steps."**
- ❏ It's time to create <u>what will be</u> put into action. What will be created, used in the learning to enhance the "3i's" of engagement and identify the supports you desire to make it a reality.
- ❏ Consider asking "Do you have an opportunity where you think you might try this in the near future?"

SEE-KS

The Mentorship Guidelines
The 6-Step Process of Appreciative Inquiry

ISCOVER
REAM
ESIGN
ELIVER

SEE-KS uses the philosophy of appreciative inquiry to guide our mentorship. A collective discussion of "what's working" fosters an ability to imagine "what might be" and the creation of the actions for "what will be." The following guidelines foster a positive, productive and emotionally regulating peer-to-peer mentorship session.

Mark-off the 6-Steps as you move through the SEE-KS appreciative inquiry process: ① ② ③ ④ ⑤ ⑥

---

① **Identify your role and review the process of appreciative inquiry.**
- ❏ Share the purpose of this mentorship opportunity and our focus on appreciating the best of what is.
- ❏ Share that we will notice the "3i's" of engagement: *investment, independence,* and *initiation.*

② **Invite the mentee(s) to start the inquiry conversation.**
- ❏ Begin by having the mentee describe the activity; what we are going to observe.
- ❏ Prompts to enhance the mentee to notice the best of <u>what is</u> might be:
  - o Can you share the learning targets or goals?
  - o Did you notice strategies that have been effective for learners' engagement?
- ❏ Share what you hear. *"So I heard you say...," "Your goals were...," "You mentioned... was working."*

③ **Discuss "what's working."**
- ❏ Use the notes gathered on the SEE-KS Mentorship Form to share <u>what is</u> noticed.
- ❏ Consider phrases that build upon what is observed to ensure appreciation *not flattery.*
  - • "I notice when ... occurs the learners demonstrate (this "3i" of engagement)."
  - • "I hear learners share ideas about personal connections to the content by saying..."
  - • "I see the learners leaning into their projects and shifting their gaze across various materials."

④ **Inquire about which of the "3i's" of engagement the mentee[s] would like to explore.**
- ❏ Imagine <u>what might be</u> by encouraging the mentee to consider ways to enhance what's working and brainstorm as if anything is possible.
- ❏ If there is uncertainty, consider asking what do you *hope for... dream for* with your learners?"

⑤ **Collaborate to discuss what possible "actions" may be to enhance what's working (10 minutes).**
- ❏ Reflect back on the notes taken in the discovery of what's working and think about <u>what could be.</u>
- ❏ Consider ways to connect the discovery of what's working with the inquiry of what might be to design learning experiences that enhance engagement, remember your hopes and dreams for learners.
- ❏ Comments might include, "I noticed when.... how might this look if...?" or "I wonder if...."

⑥ **Identify a plan and select the "next steps."**
- ❏ It's time to create <u>what will be</u> put into action. What will be created, used in the learning to enhance the "3i's" of engagement and identify the supports you desire to make it a reality.
- ❏ Consider asking "Do you have an opportunity where you think you might try this in the near future?"

Appendix F: SEE-KS Mentorship Form

 Social Emotional Engagement - Knowledge & Skills (SEE-KS)
Essential Universal Design for Learning Supports – Mentorship Form

① District / School: Educator(s):		Date: Mentor / Observer(s):	
② Subject / Lesson: Goal(s)/Target(s):	③ **What's Working** *What do you see, hear or notice?*	④ **Opportunity to enhance:** Investment / Independence / Initiation	
		⑤ **Possible Next Steps** (Generated during collaborative discussion)	
Investment can be enhanced when...			
1. Learners interests have been considered to stimulate **motivation for learning**. 2. Learners have the **supports to sustain their interest** in learning.			
Independence can be enhanced when...			
1. Learners have **access to information** presented in different ways. 2. Learners have **social expectations** presented in multiple ways.			
Initiation can be enhanced when...			
1. Learners have **options to show** what they know. 2. Learners have frequent **opportunities to share** their knowledge with others.			

⑥ **Action Plan for Next Step(s):**

SEE-KS Mentorship Steps: ① ② ③ ④ ⑤ ⑥

Appendix G: SEE-KS Mentorship Form Example

 Social Emotional Engagement - Knowledge & Skills (SEE-KS)
Essential Universal Design for Learning Supports – Mentorship Form *(2020)*

① **District / School:** Appreciation School District / Amazing School **Date:** Fall 2020
Educator(s): Ms. Rockstar **Mentor / Observer(s):** Mrs. Best-Colleague

② **Subject / Lesson:** Literacy Mini-Lesson **Goal(s)/Target(s):** Readers share their work with dramatic interpretation	③ **What's Working** *What do you see, hear or notice?*	④ **Opportunity to enhance:** Investment / Independence / Initiation ⑤ **Possible Next Steps** (generated during collaborative discussion)
Investment *can be enhanced when…*		
1. Learners interests have been considered to stimulate **motivation for learning**. 2. Learners have the **supports to sustain their interest** in learning.	• Countdown to "zero" using a fun voice from the dice generator made by learners • Learners helping to switch on and off the technology classroom board • Known peer partners from selected from an inventory done by learners • Discovery Topic: Robots energy source used to turn them on/off • Essential question posted and reviewed with the task list/agenda	How can the learners who choose not to join the lecture enhance active engagement during group discussions? How can learners access support to choose partners? **How to create meaningful & thoughtful partnerships with peers?**
Independence *can be enhanced when…*		
1. Learners have **access to information** presented in different ways. 2. Learners have **social expectations** presented in multiple ways.	• Chart paper with organizational strategy being model for students • Connecting the video on Robots to the visual organizer for the class • Option provided for some students to take their own notes at their desk, on the iPad, in a notebook. • Routine of the 3, 2, 1 , 0 lock it in phrases	How are learners' accessing the learning standards and transferring it into their work?
Initiation *can be enhanced when…*		
1. Learners have **options to show** what they know. 2. Learners have frequent **opportunities to share** their knowledge with others.	• Peers using silly voices with each other during the Think, Pair, Share related to robots video shared • Learners having inquiry time to share ideas and knowledge to peer • Freedom to seek items the room when needs were identified • Use of whiteboards, video recording and talking to share information	How is time provided for learners to learn/select their personal discovery topics based on his/her interests?

Based on the Learner Engagement Ladder data, let's explore the idea that when the learners had access to visual learning supports such as the chart paper, video, their engagement was higher (3 or 4) then when in peer partner discussions peer partner think, pair, share.

⑥ **Action Plan for Next Step(s):** Develop a think, pair share rap with visual expectations. Bring anchor chart to learners using apps such as Notability or Book-creator a) taking a photo b) share via electronic space (while song plays) c) include commenting sentence starters for sharing information with a peer.

SEE-KS Mentorship Steps: ① ② ③ ④ ⑤ ⑥

Appendix H: "3i's" of Engagement Ideas from Colleague

○	
○	
○	

References

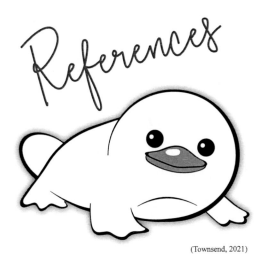

(Townsend, 2021)

THINK DIFFERENTLY:

A platypus is approximately 15 inches (38 centimeters) from its head to the end of its rump. Its tail may add an additional 5 inches (13 centimeters). The platypus weighs about 3 pounds (1.4 kilograms).

(Bradford, 2014)

Adie, L. E., Willis, J., & Van der Kleij, F. M. (2018). Diverse perspectives on student agency in classroom assessment. *Australian Educational Researcher, 45*(1), 1–12.

Banner, D., Millgårdh, J., & Olsson, M. (2010). *Minute to Win It*. Friday Television, Banner Universal Motion Pictures.

Bédard, R., & Hecker, L. (Eds.). (2020). *A spectrum of solutions for clients with autism: Treatment for adolescents and adults*. Routledge.

Bradford, A. (2014, August 4). Platypus facts. *Live Science*. https://www.livescience.com/27572-platypus.html

Brewer, J. (2020, March 10). *Making Sense Podcast: The unquiet mind.* https://open.spotify.com/show/5rgumWEx4FsqIY8e1wJNAk

Brown, B. (2018). *Dare to lead: Brave work. Tough conversations. Whole hearts.* Random House.

Brown, H. J. (2007). *Complete life's little instruction book: 1,560 suggestions, observations, and reminders on how to live a happy and rewarding life.* Thomas Nelson.

Carnegie, D. (1937). *How to win friends & influence people.* Holiday House.

CASEL. (2017). *Social emotional learning competencies.* http://CASEL.org

CAST. (2018). *Universal design for learning guidelines version 2.2.* http://CAST.org

Causton, D. J., & Macleod, D. K. (2020). *From behaving to belonging: The inclusive art of supporting students who challenge us.* ASCD.

Chevallier, C., Kohls, G., Brodkin, E. S., & Schultz, R. T. (2012). The social motivation theory of autism. *Trends in Cognitive Sciences, 16*(4), 231–239.

Cooperrider, D. L. (1990). Positive image, positive action: The affirmative basis of organizing. In S. Srivastva & D. L. Cooperrider (Eds.), *Appreciative management and leadership* (pp. 1-14). Crown Custom Publishing.

Cooperrider, D. L. (2012). *Foundational work on strengths based change.* https://www.davidcooperrider.com/speaking/

Cooperrider, D. L., & Srivastva, S. (1987). Appreciative inquiry in organizational life. In W. Pasmore & R. Woodman (Eds.), *Research in organization change and development* (Vol. 1). JAI Press.

Cooperrider, D. L., & Whitney, D. (1999). *Collaborating for change: Appreciative inquiry.* Berrett-Koehler Communications.

Csikszentmihalyi, M. (2014). Toward a psychology of optimal experience. In *Flow and the foundations of positive psychology* (pp. 209–226). Springer Netherlands.

Cunningham, K., & Shayne, D. (2020). *LEGO: Star Wars Holiday Special* [Video]. Atomic Cartoons.

DuFour, R. (Ed.). (2004). What is a professional learning community? *Educational Leadership, 61*(8), 6–11.

Dunleavy, J., & Milton, P. (2009). *What did you do in school today? Exploring the concept of student engagement and its implications for teaching and learning in Canada.* Canadian Education Association.

Durlak, J. A., Weissberg, R. P., Dymnicki, A. B., Taylor, R. D., & Schellinger, K. B. (2011). The impact of enhancing students' social and emotional learning: A meta-analysis of school-based universal interventions. *Child Development, 82,* 405–432.

Eagleman, D. (2020). *Livewired: The inside story of the ever-changing brain.* Pantheon Books.

Frijters, J., Lovett, M., Steinbach, K., Wolf, M., Sevcik, R., & Morris, R. (2011). Neurocognitive predictors of reading outcomes for children with reading disabilities. *Journal of Learning Disabilities, 44*(2), 150-166.

Hinton, C., & Fischer, K. (2008). Research schools: Grounding research in educational practice. *Mind, Brain, and Education, 2*(4), 157–160.

Joyce, B. R., & Showers, B. (1981). Transfer of training: The contribution of "coaching." *Journal of Education, 163*(2), 163–172.

Kegan, R., & Lahey, L. L. (2007). *How the way we talk can change the way we work: Seven languages for transformation.* Jossey-Bass.

Martin, B., Jr., & Carle, E. (1999). *Brown bear* (2nd ed.). Henry Holt & Company.

Metcalf, D., Metcalf, D. J., & Gargiulo, R. M. (2017). *Teaching in today's inclusive classrooms: A universal design for learning approach.* Wadsworth Cengage Learning.

Moore, S. (2018, November 5). *Don't should on me: It's not easy being NOT green* [Video]. *YouTube.* https://www.youtube.com/watch?v=MeRNhzonGts.

Rubin, E., Townsend, J., & Vittori, L. (2014). *Social Emotional Engagement Knowledge and Skills (SEE-KS).* https://www.see-ks.com/

Saggar, M., Quintin, E.-M., Bott, N. T., Kienitz, E., Chien, Y.-H., Hong, D. W.-C., & Reiss, A. L. (2016). Changes in brain activation associated with spontaneous improvisation and figural creativity after design-thinking-based training: A longitudinal fMRI study. *Cerebral Cortex, 27*(7), 3542–3552.

Schmerler, J. (2015, May 28). Don't overthink it, less is more when it comes to creativity. *Scientific American.* https://www.scientificamerican.com/article/don-t-overthink-it-

less-is-more-when-it-comes-to-creativity/

Silalahi, R. M. (2019). Understanding Vygotsky's zone of proximal development for learning. *Polyglot, 15*(2), 169.

Sinek, S. (2019). *Start with why: How great leaders inspire everyone to take action.* Penguin Business.

Townsend, B. (Graphic Designer). (2015). *SEE-KS logo* [Graphic].

UDL Exchange. (2018). http://udlexchange.cast.org

Whitman, G., & Kelleher, I. (2016). *Neuroteach: Brain science and the future of education.* Rowman & Littlefield Education.

William, J. (n.d.). Quote. *GoodReads.* https://www.goodreads.com/quotes/23215-the-deepest- principle-in-human-nature-is- the-craving-to

Willis, J. (2006). *Research based strategies to ignite student learning: Insights from a neurologist and classroom teacher.* ASCD.

Willis, J. (2007). *Brain-friendly strategies for the inclusion classroom.* ASCD.

Xiang, P., Bruene, A., & Chen, A. (2005). Research. *Journal of Teaching in Physical Education, 24*(2), 179–197.

Yoga with Adriene. (2019, September 17). http://www.yogawithadriene.com